CYCLE A GOSPEL TEXTS

FROM ASHES TO HOLY WIND

SERMONS FOR
LENT &
EASTER

F. DEAN
LUEKING

C.S.S. Publishing Co., Inc.

Lima, Ohio

FROM ASHES TO HOLY WIND

Copyright © 1989 by
The C.S.S. Publishing Company, Inc.
Lima, Ohio

Library of Congress Cataloging-in-Publication Data

Lueking, F. Dean (Frederick Dean), 1928-
From ashes to holy wind / by F. Dean Lueking.
p.   cm.
ISBN 1-55673-127-2
1. Evangelical Lutheran Church in America — Sermons. 2. Lutheran Church — Sermons. 3. Sermons, American. I. Title.
BX8066.L79F76   1989   89-15749
252.04135—dc20   CIP

9852 / ISBN 1-55673-127-2   PRINTED IN U.S.A.

Table of Contents

[1]Common Lectionary
[2]Lutheran Lectionary
[3]Roman Catholic Lectionary

Let the Journey Begin

Another Lenten journey begins this Ash Wednesday.

A Tradition to Cherish

I say, another, because for many the keeping of Lent is a treasured tradition, and these mid-week hours set aside for worship and prayer are a blessing year after year.

We journey toward Easter. The purpose of these forty days of spiritual preparation is to hail again the decisive deed of God for the redemption of the world and the renewal of our lives in Christ's grace.

May it be so for you, and for countless others of the Christian faith throughout the world.

Christ's Call to Our Inner Life

The guiding word for us as Lent begins is our Lord's call for inward soundness of spiritual life, taken from the Sermon on the Mount:

> *Beware of practicing your piety before men in order to be seen by them; for then you will have no reward from your Father who is in heaven. Thus, when you give alms, sound no trumpet before you, as the hypocrites do in the synagogues and in the streets, that they may be praised by men. Truly, I say to you, they have their reward. But when you give alms, do not let your left hand know what your right hand is doing, so that your alms may be in secret; and your Father who sees in secret will reward you. And when you pray, you must not be like the hypocrites; for they love to stand and pray in the synagogues and at the street corners, that they may be seen by men. Truly, I say to you, they have their reward. But when you pray, go into your room and shut the door and pray to your Father who is in secret; and your Father who sees in secret will reward you. And when you fast, do not look dismal, like the hypocrites, for they disfigure their faces that their*

5

fasting may be seen by men. Truly, I say to you, they have their reward. But when you fast, anoint your head and wash your face, that your fasting may not be seen by men but by your Father who is in secret; and your Father who sees in secret will reward you. Do not lay up for yourselves treasures on earth, where moth and rust consume and where thieves break in and steal, but lay up for yourselves treasures in heaven, where neither moth nor rust consumes and where thieves do not break in and steal. For where your treasure is, there will your heart be also.

(Matthew 6:1-6, 16-21)

When our thoughts turn to what is wrong in today's world and who needs changing, we consider first the cheats, drug dealers, Wall Street inside traders, and others made notorious for their broad and well-publicized wrongdoing.

He Means Us

But this word of Christ is addressed to us who come to church on Ash Wednesday. We are here because of a need for cleansing and for rededication in our lives. It is not likely that many of us deliberately turn our spirituality into an outward husk only, intentionally drying up the inner vitalities of the Spirit's handiwork in our souls. That happens unintentionally. Our minds wander when hymns are sung. The public reading of the scriptures can go right past us, with our attention never locking in to the great things proclaimed week after week. We can take it for granted that the church doors will open, the choir will sing, the clergy will preach — and all of this in a land of freedom where no one is put into jail because of worshiping God. One of the sure signs that we are drifting into routine religion is when we never talk about what goes on in worship.

The Subtlety of our Ways of Displeasing God

Jesus spoke against the blight of parading piety outwardly in ways that seem bizarre to us. After all, we do not have a brass quartet preceding us down the aisle as we make our offerings. Nor do we take our post at Lake and Harlem Streets and loudly proclaim our prayers. We're not afflicted with golden tongue orators who prattle on endlessly at the altar, "thinking that they will be heard for their many words."

Yet we do not escape the probing judgment of this text.

Not long ago I attended a convention of church people, which included a banquet for a sizeable number. I could not help but notice the people who seemed miffed because they were not assigned the more prominent seats and knew no one around their table who was *somebody*. This constant temptation to pettiness is what Jesus knows all too well. Thus he does not praise us to the skies for our flawless piety. He warns us against the pitfalls that bring sickness to the soul.

The Christ and His Cross Come First

Attending to our spiritual problems, however, is not where the primary focus for Lent is.

It is Christ himself to whom we look, and upon him we set our spiritual attention.

He consciously chose to walk the way of sorrows. This was not a display of spiritual masochism. It was in order to meet us and reach out to us in our worst moments of weakness, sin, and failure. He set his face toward Jerusalem, knowing what awaited him there, as an act of obedience to the heavenly Father's will. In giving himself totally for us, and in offering his life for our redemption from sin, the Christ comes to us with a love that makes us new from within.

The inner life is where Jesus always puts the emphasis. He does so because it is there that God aims to restore the lifeline cut by our fall into sin. The inward territory of the heart is the place that counts. That is where motive, conscience, trust, and love all are rooted. The enlivening of the inner life is the source of our freedom.

Inward Soundness, Outward Wholeness

Only when that inner life is alive in Christ can we truly fast, pray, give our offerings, speak our prayers, and serve our God without dissimulation. Then, it doesn't matter who is or who isn't looking. What matters is that we are conscious of standing before God, being accountable to him, entrusting ourselves to him, and looking only for his eye of approval upon us.

This is a great and wondrous thing, not laying up for ourselves treasures where they can rot away and consume our souls at the same time. Day after day we are pounded hard by forces which tempt us to give our all for the treasures that are earth-bound. But in our hearts we know that these things cannot ultimately satisfy.

Eager for the Journey

And so, with a deep sense of peace and hope in God, let us begin the Lenten journey. What guides us through is not what we give up, but the sacred life given for us upon the cross. Whatever we choose to lay aside and do without, let God alone know and refrain from broadcasting the word around. Lenten living that responds to this text is in large part a hidden journey to those with whom we share the journey. But that is as it should be. All hinges upon the Father's knowing us and our knowing the Father.

With our souls secured by Christ, and with faces lit with hope and a holy joy we:

. . . run with perseverance the race that is set before us, looking to Jesus the pioneer and perfecter of our faith, who for the joy that was set before him endured the cross, despising the shame, and is seated at the right hand of the throne of God.

(Hebrews 12:1-2)

Tempter and Tempted

Then Jesus was led up by the Spirit into the wilderness to be tempted by the devil. And he fasted forty days and forty nights, and afterward he was hungry. And the tempter came and said to him, "If you are the Son of God, command these stones to become loaves of bread." But he answered, "It is written, 'Man shall not live by bread alone, but by every word that proceeds from the mouth of God.' " Then the devil took him to the holy city, and set him on the pinnacle of the temple and said to him, "If you are the Son of God, throw yourself down; for it is written, 'He will give his angels charge of you,' and 'On their hands they will bear you up, lest you strike your foot against a stone.' " Jesus said to him, "Again it is written, 'You shall not tempt the Lord your God.' " Again, the devil took him to a very high mountain, and showed him all the kingdoms of the world and the glory of them; and he said to him, "All these I will give you, if you will fall down and worship me." Then Jesus said to him, "Begone, Satan! for it is written, 'You shall worship the Lord your God and him only shall you serve.' " Then the devil left him, and behold, angels came and ministered to him.

Two Figures Meet in the Desert

Tempter and tempted meet in the wilderness, St. Matthew tells us. Let every ounce of your imagination trace those two figures on the landscape of the Judean desert. Let the location sink in. To this day, the region south and east of Jerusalem retains its rugged and desolate terrain. There is an immense stillness about that desert. Barren land, rock, and sky come together to form a scene that is both eerie and awesome. It is there that the Spirit led Jesus up, into the wilderness, to be tempted by the devil.

The Where of the Temptation

Why should this geographical detail be included in the Gospel account of that struggle with nothing less than the destiny of humankind at stake? The wilderness solitude is not incidental at all.

It signifies the human heart, which is always the main location of the Tempter's onslaught. We learn something essential about temptation by means of this detail about this text.

Temptation is usually regarded as being "out there." We warn our children about the company they keep, steering them clear of bad actors. We adults think about the temptation of great amounts of money. Or someone else's body. Or the bottle. Or seductive fame. These are the things that are temptation. Always out there.

The Battle Begins in our Heart

To be sure, these things do pose danger. But the reason why we fall for them is because of what is in here, in the inner heart of our own life. The Tempter did not lead Jesus down some Bourbon Street, or along Wall Street, or around the Pentagon (sex, money, power) in order to set the stage of his attack. He encountered Jesus in the solitude of the wilderness, where there was nothing on the landscape or in the surroundings that would confuse the issue. The Tempter knows this about us: the region of the heart and soul is where he directs his aim. "Out of the heart proceed murder, theft, adultery, etc . . ." our Lord said. The heart is at odds with God, as today's First Lesson from Genesis 2 teaches. Our first parents made the wrong choice with their freedom, to be "like God." That meant no need for God. Their story is our story.

And so we are all capable of being tempted, simply by being alive. We can't run off to a monastery to escape, for we always carry our soul with us. Who is temptable? All of us. All the time.

The What of Temptation

The first of the three attacks by the Tempter on the one tempted takes place. Jesus had fasted forty days and nights, and his body was weakened with hunger. That is an experience very few of us know anything about first hand. But there are others in our world who know the month of March to be the time of hunger, since the granary has emptied and the new crops have not yet produced. Hunger is a terrible ordeal, making the human body vulnerable to every other assault of disease besides withering the spirit. Jesus knew that hunger.

Bread First, or Word First?

"If you are the Son of God, turn these stones into bread." In what does the first temptation consist? Not theological arguments over the existence of God, or urgent ethical matters of right or wrong. The first temptation deals with fundamental existence, survival itself. The appeal is so plausible!

After all, says the Enemy, you are the Son of God. Now let that sonship be manifested by turning these desert stones into bread. After all, as we often hear it said, good health is everything. Sacrifice that and everything else is a moot question.

But Jesus meets that temptation with the scriptural word, "Man shall not live by bread alone but by every word that proceeds from the mouth of God." Of course humans need food. But Jesus saw that the Tempter was choosing the grounds on which to posit the matter of what comes first in our existence. His response puts first and foremost the living God, who speaks to his creation and offers the word of truth and grace for us all. All temptation aims to obscure that central truth, that God has the first claim upon our hearts.

It is not our job, not food or shelter, not clothing or family — it is God who alone can occupy the center places of our hearts. Bread, received in faith, is given us by God so that we will trust ourselves completely to his Word. In an affluent society such as our own, this cannot be overemphasized. Terrifically strong forces of temptation pound away at our hearts, attempting to enthrone some thing or person other than God as sovereign there. Jesus met that force at its source. It is he whom we call Lord. He has struggled with the Tempter on our behalf. We need none less than him to keep us in the time when we are tempted to believe that humans do, indeed, live by bread alone.

The Temptation of Holy Things

The second temptation Jesus met was at the holy city, on the holy temple, with the holy word spoken by the Tempter. How different the scene of the second from the first temptation! "If you are the Son of God, cast yourself down . . ." From the lofty pinnacle of the temple where the Tempter had led him, Jesus faced the attack which uses holy things. The Enemy quotes Psalm 91, with every appearance of reverence for that passage which says that God will give his angels charge over us, lest we dash our foot against a stone.

Here, the essence of temptation is to turn religion into spectacle. What could be more dramatic, more spectacular proof of the providence of God than to step off the temple parapet into thin air, with Psalm 91 on his lips? Is not this an appeal to the God who does miracles, who defies the laws of gravity, who intervenes against all odds and snatches his anointed one from disaster? Isn't that what God is supposed to do — go against the normal course of events in order to show who he is?

Thus is religion turned from ultimate trust in God into spurious reliance on the miraculous. A well-known religious figure announces that he must raise millions of dollars by the end of March or God will strike him dead. How much more bombastic can one get? All this obscures the real nature of God who does not depend on spectacles to recommend himself. His power is not demonstrated in defiance of the laws of nature he himself has authored. He knows every sparrow that falls, every hair of our heads, every cry of need from our hearts. He is the God of mercy and long suffering, not bombastic entertainment that dazzles the mind momentarily but never changes the heart.

"You shall not tempt the Lord your God," is Jesus' reply. Jesus met the temptation to misuse religion by trusting the holy, redemptive will of the heavenly Father. All quoting of the Bible that seeks some other end is the devil's work. Dump it.

The Temptation of Power, and Its Glory

Now comes the final temptation, in which Jesus is led up a very high mountain and shown the kingdoms of the world and their glory. "All this I will give you . . ." says Satan.

Before our Lord's eyes there were marching armies, fluttering banners, masses of people in adulation of the power that rules them. Think of it — the whole world and all its glory — for Christ. Who among us knows absolutely nothing of the lure of power, the magic of being able to give commands, order people, occupy the place of authority?

"All this I will give you . . ." Satan says, and then turns his head away so that Jesus might not hear the rest of that fatuous promise, ". . . if you will fall down and worship me." Just one pinch of incense, only one split second of compromise — that's all the Tempter asked. Jesus' answer whips him around, "You shall worship the Lord your God and him only shall you serve."

In that fateful moment, when the kingdoms of this world and their glory were set before the Son of God, he chose the other way. The kingdom of God he ushered in does not establish itself by brute force, or cunning deals, or inquisitions, or crusades, or mighty armies and all the arsenals that one superpower struts against the other (I speak of the United States of America and the Soviet Union).

Not by Might, Nor by Power . . .

Jesus kept his eye upon another place. We know it is Golgotha, and there he took up his lonely cross on our behalf. There one of the kingdoms of this world was instrumental in putting him to death. But Rome did not win. Nor will any nation or empire, including our own. God brings his Kingdom in by forgiving the sins of the world through his Son who carried our guilt on his back and paid for our guilt with his lifeblood. He lives to ever make intercession for us, especially when we are tempted to put our flag over his Cross — at the expense of justice, truth, and love. The sad spectacle of

"Irangate" is one more reminder that all the efforts to rule by force over other peoples, totally oblivious to their real needs of bread for the soul and body, can have no other end than disaster. Lives are ruined. People are dismayed. Trust is broken. Suffering goes on. It was against all this that Jesus put himself in this last temptation.

In all of literature, there is hardly a more riveting scene than in that section of Feodor Dostoyevsky's *The Brothers Karamazov*. It is based on the temptation of Jesus. It is the time of the Spanish Inquisition in the fifteenth-century in Seville. Jesus appears among the poor, harassed, suffering people, and ministers to them. The Grand Inquisitor, who had just ordered heretics burned at the stake, summons Jesus. He taunts Jesus, claiming that he never understood the need of people for bread, spectacle, authority. Jesus is accused of setting impossible standards, totally out of reach of the compromised, mortal, begging people who clamor every day for bread, for entertainment, for someone to give them all the answers. Jesus will not bend to the Grand Inquisitor. And once more, Jesus is sent off condemned.

Our Lenten Journey

That moment in literature is replayed in real life daily. All of us live under temptation. Forgetting that subjects us to the greatest temptation, of all to think there is none. Then we go into every day with airy oblivion to the dark forces that swirl around us.

On this first Sunday in Lent, behold the man! See him locked in mortal struggle with Satan whose face we never can see but whose work of destruction we can see. He is the one who sends his Spirit to keep guard over our hearts, and to do for us what we can never do for ourselves: secure our hearts. He is a Lord who knows temptation, yet without sinning. In our time of testing, in any hour when despair threatens us, let us draw near his throne of grace and find mercy to help in time of need.

1st Sunday after Pentecost B
(The Holy Trinity)

Let God Be God

What an Immense Privilege is Ours!

Today it is with an especially deep sense of gratitude and humility that I preach the text chosen for this sermon. Think of it — we come together in faith, health, and freedom to worship the living God. He welcomes us. He knows us by name. He invites us to know him by name. These are all wondrous and momentous gifts. Just to be able to know God and to proclaim the truth of his being here among us and his being for us is the first privilege of life.

At times we are tempted to try to explain God. But if God were so easily comprehended in our human explanation, he would not be God. At the other end of the spectrum, God is not so remote as to leave us speechless. He does come to us and will always leave his witness among us. The third chapter of John's Gospel is where we find our textual bearings for the proclamation today:

> *Now there was a man of the Pharisees, named Nicodemus, a ruler of the Jews. This man came to Jesus by night and said to him, "Rabbi, we know that you are a teacher come from God; for no one can do these signs that you do, unless God is with him." Jesus answered him, "Truly, truly, I say to you, unless one is born anew, he cannot see the kingdom of God." Nicodemus said to him, "How can a man be born when he is old? Can he enter a second time into his mother's womb and be born?" Jesus answered, "Truly, truly, I say to you, unless one is born of water and the Spirit, he cannot enter the kingdom of God. That which is born of the flesh is flesh, and that which is born of the Spirit is spirit. Do not marvel that I said to you, 'You must be born anew.' The wind blows where it wills, and you hear the sound of it, but you do not know whence it comes or whither it goes; so it is with every one who is born of the Spirit." Nicodemus said to him, "How can this be?" Jesus answered him, "Are you a teacher of Israel, and yet you do not understand this? Truly, truly, I say to you, we speak of what we know, and bear witness to what we have seen; but you do not receive*

15

our testimony. If I have told you earthly things and you do not believe, how can you believe if I tell you heavenly things? No one has ascended into heaven but he who descended from heaven, the Son of man. And as Moses lifted up the serpent in the wilderness, so must the Son of man be lifted up, that whoever believes in him may have eternal life." For God so loved the world that he gave his only Son, that whoever believes in him should not perish but have eternal life. For God sent the Son into the world, not to condemn the world, but that the world might be saved through him.

(John 3:1-17)

The Nighttime Seeker

It has often been noted that Nicodemus came to Jesus by night, out of fear of being found out. No doubt he did come with concern that some of his fellow Pharisees might see him and report his visit. But the point is that he came. He came with a sense of searching and desire to know more of this unconventional rabbi from Galilee who was performing such signs as Jerusalem had not seen before.

Jesus gave Nicodemus far more than the man was seeking. Before the conversation is two or three sentences along, it is clear that our Lord is taking the subject to heights and depths his visitor had never dreamed of.

God the Sovereign One

Jesus speaks first of that rich Old Testament theme — the Kingdom of God. Basic here is the truth that God is sovereign. He is King. He is Ruler and Lord, Creator and God of all. To enter into relationship with God, to be a part of his Kingdom, is likened to birth — or rather, re-birth. Belonging to God is receiving his life. That is what God's Kingdom means — his active ruling in the lives of those who are his children by faith.

The Mystery of the Spirit's Work

Then Jesus tells Nicodemus of the mystery of God's Spirit. Like the wind, which no one of us perceives as to its origin and outcome, so the Spirit of God moves and works. The Spirit makes it possible for that which is born as flesh to be born anew as spiritually alive. The Spirit of God is God's presence, creating interest and awareness of the spiritual base for life. The Spirit creates faith in us, and causes that faith to motivate us to love and serve God freely.

The Uplifted Messiah

It is Jesus who is teaching these truths. He then goes on to speak of himself as the Son of man, descended from Heaven, and lifted up that all who believe in him might be saved. In testifying thus to himself, Jesus puts his own life and being into the continuity of the action of God in revealing himself. The sovereign God has come to the world supremely in his messianic Son, who willingly suffered death on an uplifted Cross for the redemption of the world. Through the mystery of the Spirit, this truth comes alive in all who receive the gift of grace and respond in faith.

One God, Three Ways of His Coming to Us

The one God comes to us three fold in his revelation: sovereign Creator, messianic Son, life-giving Spirit. All this is in the text from John 3. The word Triune or Trinity does not occur. That word came along later in the church's vocabulary. It is not found in the Bible. Yet the truth of God to which the word points is found throughout the Bible. For that reason, we call ourselves believers in the Triune God. The point of such language is to be faithful to God's own way of revealing himself. Like all our human language, it falls short in reaching its goal. Still, we speak! With regard to God, surely our speech needs to be seasoned with humility as well as with confidence that God who is eternal yet chooses to dwell among us and be known by us.

Throughout the centuries, Christians have striven to express this Triune understanding of the oneness of God's being in various ways. The underlying belief is that God's very being is reflected in his creation. Augustine spoke of the mind, with its capacity for memory, understanding, and will. One mind — yet active in threefold ways. John of Damascus was one among many early church fathers who spoke of water that bubbled up from a spring, flowed into a river, and reached its source in the ocean. Water is one, yet spring, river, and ocean are distinctive expressions of it. Luther spoke of the root, trunk, and fruit of a tree as he ruminated on the way the living God is traceable in his creation. He spoke of iron in a blacksmith's shop that would glow, burn, and place its stamp on wood.

All these efforts to help us in our understanding of God do not explain him in completeness, of course. Nor are they meant to. They keep us mindful of a mystery — that one essence comes through to us in a tri-fold fashion. That is what the ancients meant when they spoke of the persons of the Godhead — person means a way of existence, a way of showing forth the main thing.

God is Love

The main thing, the one thing, that God wants to make known to us is that he is love. Nothing God ever reveals of himself is apart from his love. That is why the text from John 3 reaches its climax in this great affirmation: "God so loved the world that he gave his only Son, that whoever believes in him might not perish but have eternal life."

This is a truth that brings us good news. Receiving the revelation of God's being means rejoicing that our sins are forgiven, and that there is hope for people throughout the world because the Son of man has been lifted up upon the cross for us all. I tell you that Gospel again today: God comes to us. He is for us. Never mind that there are the unsearchable depths of his wisdom and his being; that truth must not make God more remote. He is our Savior. His Spirit is our comforter. We call God — Father, dear Father. These truths revealed move us to sing and pray and put his love to work in the lives we live.

Displacing Our Idols

Nicodemus came to Jesus with a heart and mind already well-furnished with concepts, ideas, assumptions, and convictions. He was a Jew, and well-trained in the revelation God gave to Abraham, Isaac, and Jacob of old.

No one is a total spiritual vacuum.

Everyone has something or someone that has been placed into that inner spiritual center of our lives where God intends to reign. Our trouble is that we put someone or something other than God at the center. When that happens, and it does each day, we must face the results. Some time ago the whole world was given a glimpse of what happens when people give soccer teams god-like importance. When a team so passionately supported lost a key match, some of its supporters went on a binge of rioting that left thirty-eight people dead. That news event tells us something about what happens in life when God is not God for people. The gods we bring in are so cruel. When the idols crash down within us, those we have established by our own will and making, we are crushed. Idols are absolutely heartless and colder than any ice water in our veins.

Much closer to home, Charles Colson has some observations on our culture. Remember Colson? He was a presidential aide under Richard Nixon, a man who had a six-figure income, a yacht, an office next to the President in the White House, and nearly unlimited power. Colson used all that as an idol, and went to prison for it finally. But his life has been turned around by the Kingdom of God revealed in Christ through the mystery of the Holy Spirit. He devoted himself full-time to ministry to those in prison. More recently, however, he spoke of yuppies in America as a mirror of our idolatry. He read designer t-shirt lines: "The one who dies with the most toys wins," or "Nuclear war? What about my career?" He sees these sophisticated witticisms as bearers of the false gods that are set up when people make half-truths into whole truths by which to live. Colson tells us that it is idolatrous to believe that life is defined by what we own, or that money is the source of all good. The self-serving lifestyle that grows out of these idolatries is banal, boring, and ultimately suffocating. God doesn't want our successes. He wants us. He does not demand our achievements. He calls for our obedience.

Safeguards and Stretching Us

Letting God be God puts safeguards on our constant tendency, as Christians and people of the church, to veer off into bypaths. One way of making this point about safeguards that the Triune God gives us is to see the problem of unitarianisms.

Unitarianism of the first person of the blessed Trinity means regarding God as the creator of all, to be sure, but keeping him at a comfortable distance. It is a nature religion, agreeing mentally that God has put the world together and no doubt he keeps it going. But this religious view never gets us to our knees, in adoration and love for God our Father. It also sets us up for assuming that God is mainly active among people like us in color and status, and his favor rests upon nations that turn out to be compatible with the United States. We need to be safeguarded against that kind of unitarianism by keeping before us God's work through Jesus Christ his Son and the Holy Spirit.

Unitarianism of the second person of the blessed Trinity means making Jesus Savior in our lives, to be sure. But it shrivels Jesus' saving work into something that is far short of the universal lordship of the Son of God throughout creation. It is possible to get comfortable with a Jesus-and-me-alone religion which is closed to the care of creation or to the unifying work of the Holy Spirit in gathering Christ's people into congregations of imperfect people with plenty of problems to solve. We need the stretching, safeguarding work of the Triune God to spare us the problem of narrowing God's work in Christ to the exclusion of his creation and its care, his sanctifying and its meaning for the church.

Unitarianism of the third person of the blessed Trinity means so concentrating upon the work of the Holy Spirit that we lose sight of the central place of the Cross and the fatherly work of God in creation. The problem here is making our own subjective feelings and experience central instead of subservient. No Christian can feel constant exaltation and know constant victory. We're mashed flat sometimes, and it is very humbling. We need safeguarding against a unitarianism of the Holy Spirit, and stretching to the work of the Father and the Son as well as to the Holy Spirit.

Best Seen on Our Knees

Our best response to the truth of the living God comes not in talking about him, but in responding to him — with love and gratitude and humility.

Do you want to see the living God? Look for him in the lives of his people. See him in the beauty of his creation. Catch the signs of his Spirit in the greater beauty of faith-filled people.

I conclude as I began, with emphasis upon the wonder and greatness of God who does such a daring thing as give himself to us and our world. That is his choice, and in his so choosing and so doing, our salvation is secured. Blessed be the Father and the Son and the Holy Spirit, now and forever.

A Moment of Brightness

And after six days Jesus took with him Peter and James and John his brother, and led them up a high mountain apart. And he was transfigured before them and his face shone like the sun and his garments became white as light.
(Matthew 17:1-2)

In these words the evangelist Matthew tells us of a transcendent moment in the ministry of our Lord.

Where It Occurred

It is noteworthy that Jesus went to a quiet place of welcome remoteness, and that he took with him the three disciples closest to him. The Transfiguration did not occur on a busy street in Jerusalem, nor in the household of Mary and Martha, nor even while ministering to the sick and dying. There is a clue for us to heed in the fact that Jesus changed the pace and the place of his work for a brief interlude of rest and retreat. He needed that. We do, too. It calls to our attention the importance of taking time and making room in our crowded schedules for quiet places, conducive to prayer and uninterrupted attention to God. ". . . He led them up a high mountain apart . . ." is a quiet invitation for us to seek times and places where we, too, are apart from all the things which distract us and pre-empt our energies of spirit and body.

How This Moment Fits In

Some biblical scholars have written that the Transfiguration of Jesus may be a misplaced part of the Easter narrative, that it happened after and not before his Resurrection. There is no warrant for such speculation,

21

however. We do well to leave it where it is in Matthew's Gospel. It occurred before Christ's passion.

The Glory Given the Son

What happened to him is more, certainly, than the evangelist can express and we can comprehend. It was a profound and glorious moment for our Lord. It is to be understood by us as another link in the chain of epiphanies whereby the heavenly Father revealed himself in his Son. The moment was rich in symbols. His face shone like the sun; his garments reflected that radiance in such a way as to have a brightness of their own. A bright cloud surrounded him, so reminiscent of Old Testament epiphanies of God's glory. The cloud is the biblical symbol of God's holy presence, and it is his luminous presence that filled the night with a sacred brightness. Matthew tells us that the divine voice was heard (but by any save Jesus himself?), affirming his Son as the one in whom he is pleased. It is to him that we are to listen.

Old Testament Fulfilled

Moses and Elijah appear and each is portrayed as talking with Jesus. Both Old Testament figures have an air of mystery about their departure from this life. No one knew Moses' burial place. Elijah was taken into God's presence in the fiery chariot. But it is Jesus who remains the central figure in the Transfiguration. Concerning his death there is to be no mystical shroud. His death is coming, and it is indeed public! His resurrection is the central theme of the entire New Testament, toward which all else points — including his Transfiguration.

What This Moment Points To

The moment of brightness on the mountain with his closest trio of disciples prepared our Lord for another mountain. At the place called Golgotha his face was not wrapped in radiance, but rather with bloody sweat. The disciples all deserted him at the Cross, which is worse by far than blurting out such an out-of-place sentence as Peter's clumsy suggestion about the booths. At Calvary there was no divine voice heard, only Jesus' cry of forsakenness. Yet it is that moment which was truly his glory. It was for that moment ("hour" as the Gospel of John refers to it) that he came into the world.

The bright moment of Transfiguration strengthened our Lord, confirmed him as the divine Son, and prepared him for the fulfillment of his mission. We hear this text today, near the beginning of the Lenten season. It fits into the larger pattern of Christ's whole ministry in this way: God prepared his Son for the task given him. No trial came to the Son for which the Father had not prepared him.

The Father's Love Enfolds All of Us

The manner in which the Father loved his Son is the revelation of that love for all his sons and daughters of all time and all places. Listen, then, to him. And "behold what manner of love the Father has shown us, that we should be called his sons and daughters."

In listening to the Christ of the Transfiguration, we can benefit greatly in respect to two aspects of our own lives.

Set No Boundaries on Him

First, the Transfiguration serves to widen our spiritual horizon as to who Christ is for us. It warns us against taking him for granted. It gives us reason to stop in our tracks, and stand in awe of him who reveals to us the overwhelming greatness of God's very being. It is a problem peculiar to church members, who have long known the catechism and hymns and Scriptures, to "localize" Jesus in our own experience of the tradition about him. It does happen, usually without our being conscious of it, that we box him in, tag him, and file him away in our own set of spiritual experiences. This is not to say at all that everything we have ever known or experienced of him is wrong by any means. The problem is when we slip into assuming that our grasp of his fullness is complete, and that he is nothing more than what we have known of him.

I have in mind — uncomfortably so — an experience at a church convention many years ago. A crowd of people were at the door of the conference hall, waiting to receive materials for the next session. I was talking with a person wearing a button (what is a convention delegate without a button?) which was an ingenious design in black and white — spelling out the name of our Lord. But the design of the name JESUS was such that one had to look twice, maybe three times, to discern the name. It was a kind of riddle. The artist intended it that way. One could not recognize the name immediately and then hurry on to some other things. A kind of curiosity was aroused, the further inquiry invited. Then — perhaps with a word of explanation — the real meaning of the symbol became apparent.

But one lady standing alongside us spied that button and reddened with anger. She directed her question to the button-wearer, "Why do you cover up my Jesus?" I have no idea what kind of button would have plesed her — maybe a battery-powered number that would blink out the message in neon lights: "JESUS . . . JESUS . . . JESUS." Her angry question about "my Jesus" made me want to shoot back an answer, ". . . because, lady, there is more to Jesus than you ever dreamed. He's not just your Jesus.

You don't have him all to yourself, locked into your own style and experience. For God's sake, woman (literally, for the sake of God), make room in your mind and soul for the mystery, the glory, the transcendence of our Lord.'' That's what I felt like saying.

But I didn't. It doesn't matter what was said or not said then.

But this is the point now. God forbid that you and I as individual Christians, or our congregation, or our part of the whole family of God fall into the trap of resenting anything and everything that stretches us toward new hints of his glory and the fuller stature of his Sonship. The Transfiguration tells us to stand before him in awe. We miss that altogether if we have him all figured out, packaged in our wrapper, covered over in our smugness.

Against Spiritual Egoism

The second point of the Transfiguration speaks to an opposite problem.

There is such a thing as being so enchanted by the mystery and glory of Christ that all we want is that enchantment.

This was Peter's problem. In one of the classic "foot-in-mouth disease" lines in the New Testament, Peter has to say something about how nice it is to be present at such a splendid moment and would it not be fine to set up three booths to preserve the whole glorious thing for the rest of time.

Peter, like many of us clergy, thought that every sacred moment required comment. When that happens, the blessing of silence is ruined, of course. I once heard a seasoned Christian of India express his amazement over our western church ways of announcing at the beginning of an hour of worship, "The Lord is in his holy temple, let all within keep silence" and then following that call to worship with sixty minutes of uninterrupted speech.

The central point is: the moment of brightness is not the only moment in the life of faith. We are on the wrong track if we think that solid, growing faith produces non-stop spiritual exaltation.

We need to be reminded that there is such a thing as holy tedium in our practice of the faith and in our worship of the living God. Expect it. Don't resent it. We say the same things so often in our liturgy. We repeat the same Psalms, offer the same prayers day after day, and keep on resorting to what our forefathers have handed down to us. To be sure, God's mercies are new every morning and his love is ever unchanging. But our experiences of it may not be constantly bright and transfiguring, simply because we are mortal and not yet complete in our sanctification. The new song is also an old song, and the flame of the Spirit which still burns in our souls is the age-old flame which through the ages has burned in every place and shown the glory of God to a dark world.

A Message for This Moment of American Life

Do not seek spiritual experience for its own sake. Nor do we need to constantly compare our pattern of spiritual vitality with the experiences of others. Our present time in American church life is rich and varied in charismatic experience and born-again testimony. I rejoice in the Spirit's renewing power in the lives of all God's people. But none of us need conclude that we stay on the Mount of Transfiguration all our waking hours. There is the duty of walking over humdrum ground, the duty of bearing with boring people, the duty of going through periods of spiritual experience that are not illumined by ever-new revelations but which are sustained by the memory of bright moments of Christ's presence before.

Jim Wallis analyzed American culture in these words:

> Self-satisfaction and self-fulfillment are the undisputed gods and the unrivaled idols of American culture at the moment. Thus far the present evangelical revival has shown a characteristically evangelical preference for proclaiming personal spiritual experience while ignoring the biblical standards of social justice and righteousness. The leading question of too many of us is what Jesus can do for me, how he can make me happier, more successful, more content, more prosperous. It may be that we are living in one of the most shallow and self-serving periods in all of church history.

I take Wallis seriously, because I respect him as a committed Christian who speaks from within the tradition he criticizes. We all need that counsel, since so much of our pilgrimage is down from the mountain and squarely in the middle of routine duties and responsibilities of our discipleship.

But having said that, let us heed the moment of brightness our Lord received from his Father, and welcome such moments of brightness as he may be pleased to grant as we travel from heights to depths and on to our goal of life eternal.

John 4:5-26 (27-42) (C)   *Lent 3*
John 4:5-26 (27-30, 39-42) (L)   *Lent 2*
John 4:5-42 (RC)   *Lent 3*

Wellspring for the Soul

When Water is Scarce

Some time ago I had an experience unique in my life — living in a place for several weeks where no drinking water was piped in. On the western edge of Kenya I learned what it is to go to the village well, draw water for two buckets, and carry them back to the small house where our family was living. The African women at the well always wanted me to do it their way — carry the bucket on my head. I have neither the balance that takes, nor enough hair to give a water bucket much support.

How easily we take water for granted. In our part of the world all we need to do is turn a water faucet and out it comes — clean, safe, drinkable, life-giving water. If only all the people in the world had that privilege! A good way to begin hearing this text today is to remember to be thankful to the Creator for the abundance of water he gives us.

A Weary Lord by Jacob's Well

Jesus knew the welcome refreshment of cool well water on a hot noonday hour in a dusty place in Samaria. Jacob's well is where the text from John 4 places him. It was famous for centuries as the place where the patriarch Jacob had found water. It was part of the land that Jacob had given to his son Joseph. (The well is still there today, about an hour's drive north of Jerusalem.)

He was tired when he came to that well-known stopping place between Jerusalem and Galilee. His exit from Jerusalem had been hurried and trouble-filled as he was forced to leave Jerusalem because of the fury of the opposition there. His disciples had gone to the town of Sychar for food when our Lord met another lone visitor to the well.

27

Meeting a Deeper Thirst

She came without friends, at an hour when most of the other women of the town would not be present at the well. Perhaps she was alone because her reputation was jaded — going through five husbands and taking to her bed now a man not her husband does not suggest a woman of strong moral character. Jesus asked her for a drink of water; she was surprised that he would speak to her at all — relations between Jews and Samaritans being as hostile as they were. Jesus replied in a cryptic way, telling her of a "living water which does not give out" that he had and wished to offer. Here is the verse of the text that is before us today:

Every one who drinks of this water will thirst again, but whoever drinks of the water that I shall give him will never thirst; the water I shall give him will become in him a spring of water welling up to eternal life.

(John 4:14)

None of us should fault the woman for being at a loss in hearing such words. Nor is it so strange that she would want to turn the conversation away from her past marriages. She cannot make connections at any point with what Jesus wanted her to understand and to receive from him. His words and her responses kept going back and forth at different levels altogether.

Where can we begin to find ourselves in this text? Surely the evangelist does not mean to simply leave us as observers of a strange conversation a very long time ago. How can the word come forth to us from the words of this narrative in the fourth chapter of St. John?

When Our Souls Run Dry

All of us experience times of spiritual dryness, when we know that life is not all that it could be, when we settle into grooved pathways of life that make our inner landscape of soul something like the pictures we see of parched desert land. It does not surprise me that this text tells of one who was no doubt in her middle years of life — or maybe beyond. Much is written about the problem of stagnating seasons of life, when the well runs dry on the inside. Not so long ago a wife came in to speak to me of her puzzlement over her husband who has just seemed to have lost his grip on life. What disturbs her most is not just his outward indifference to the marriage, the family, the job. It is his inner listlessness of soul that gives her concern. The medieval church had a word for this ailment — *accidie* they called it in Latin. It means a sloth — a kind of drought of soul, sadness in the face of spiritual good, a sort of "so what?" outlook that concludes that since nothing counts, anything goes. Prayer dries up. Values are held but loosely if at all. Life grows dull. Hope seems pointless. Love is just too much work.

Recovering a Buried Desire

What one doesn't even realize under such a cover of spiritual dryness is that a thirst for life and freshness of spirit and purpose under God is still there. Like the Samaritan woman, we become oblivious to the innermost vacuum of our souls and as a result can't even recognize our real malady anymore. The slow, relentless winding down of spiritual vitality continues and we miss its signs. And suddenly the Savior's words which may have once caught hold of us like a clear, commanding voice are incomprehensible. Indeed, there is no thirst for his word anymore. There's no thirst for much of anything.

It is to that rocky contour of our inner life that Jesus brings this astounding Word of his. He himself is the wellspring that never runs dry, keeps on gushing up in a living stream of life-giving water that continues into eternal life.

Wellspring

There is such a water. He is that water. It won't do to just describe the problem of how life flattens out into desert places of the soul. What is called for now in your life and mine is a sizing up of where we are and what is offered to us in the Son of God who loved us and gave himself for us. The water of life he brings us is salvation. It is the blessing of his cross and the power of his resurrection. That Gospel is the renewing, empowering gift of Christ who dug so deeply into the soil of our dry souls to touch the final stratum of our need. What refreshment there is in grace for sinners!

Where Life-Giving Waters Flow

In my own life I keep finding that the wellspring of the Gospel comes through to me in the actual relationships with people in the daily ministry. There is a miracle of the Holy Spirit involved in the personal interaction with people. Finding that Christ is present in people as we meet them in faith is finding a constant source of refreshment, renewal, and the restoring of spiritual energy in the soul. I hope you find that to be true for you as well.

The Beginning of New Beginnings

It is noteworthy that the end of this passage (John 4:27-30) shows us this Samaritan woman in animated conversation with her neighbors in Sychar, telling them of Jesus and all the things he had said to her. She doesn't fully grasp their meaning yet. But she speaks and acts like a woman who has taken a deep drink at a fresh water well that renews her. She is no longer alone; community is beginning to mean something to her again. She doesn't dismiss the strange Jew at the well as a somewhat deranged person; she is at the early stages of belonging to him in a faith she never dreamed could be her own. Her life is no longer one day after another, back and forth to the well for water for that day. A parched soul has had life-giving water poured onto it. She is beginning to learn what it can mean to live from the wellspring of grace which Christ Jesus is.

Sometimes Like a Winterbourne

That same experience is meant for us. Life can become unbearably commonplace and dried up as far as our eternal destiny is concerned. But the Gospel of God's grace in Christ Jesus for sinners begins to have its way in us, like a tiny rivulet of flowing water beneath tons of ice and snow. Such a barely-visible movement of water is called a "winterbourne." It is hardly discernible, but it's there. And as it continues to flow, the icy mass which seems to choke it, gradually gives way. The tons of debris do not quench the winterbourne; that tiny stream finally melts away the ice mass over it. Let that truth help you today if you find it hard to rejoice in the promises of God, if Jesus' word to you about himself as the living water seems distant and quite unreal. We cannot make that word speak to us with waters of life. We can only ask the giver to make it so. Do that! Press on in your plea to God to be the wellspring of living water he promises to be. (Revelation 21:6)

Sometimes Like a Waterfall

And there are times when the wellspring of Christ's goodness flows into us and through us to others like a Niagara Falls. If that is how it is with you now, be grateful. You are experiencing just what God the Creator made you to experience. There is nothing more splendid and lasting in its goodness than "tasting and seeing that the Lord is good." (Psalm 34:8) Don't depend on anything or anyone else to be that wellspring except our blessed Lord himself. Certainly, we find refreshment in all that is good, beautiful, and true. But God's gifts cannot be for us what he the giver is. Trust him with your heart, and drink deeply at the wellspring of his grace in Christ Jesus.

There is an unmistakable freshness about the lives of those who do so. There is such a need for those people in the world around us today. Let me mention one example of such a need.

One Special Need for Spiritually Freshened Lives

It has to do with the calling of public school teachers in our land. In general, the assessment is that public education is in deep trouble, especially in the schools in the cities of America. We don't hear too often of young people who are aspiring to be public school teachers in the inner cities of the country. The unspoken feeling is that there is too much violence, too much distraction, too much indifference on the part of everybody to make teaching worthwhile.

From time to time a call goes out to restore prayer in the classrooms of the nation. Public school teachers cannot be called upon to lead prayers that have to be so generalized, so disconnected from conviction, so isolated from the community of living faith. It is right to desire spiritual good for masses of public school children. But this is not the method. The public school classroom cannot be the place of genuine spiritual renewal that issues into faithful prayer.

I propose another view, and it comes out of my own experiences as one who went to public schools up to the college level of my life. The teachers who were men and women of integrity, of undisputable character and spiritual soundness made a difference in my life by being the people they were. They blessed me, not in writing prayer necessarily addressed: "To Whom It May Concern." The leaven of their lives consisted in their dedication to children, to skill and high degree of motivation. They did not just have a job. They gave themselves to us as people in a high calling. Not all public school teachers were like that in my youth — or anyone's. But there were enough to make a life-long difference to me. We have public school teachers present in this worship today and every Sunday. You have a high calling under God. As you carry it out, well-nourished again today by Christ the wellspring of your soul, you perform for children today what I am describing.

The Wellspring Who Does Not Fail

"As the deer pants for the waterbrook, so my soul thirsts for the living God" the Psalmist sings. (42:1) We all have that deep thirst to be met. The water of life is ever fresh and suffficient as it comes to us from that same Lord who sat down by a well of Jacob long ago, and led a dried-up life to wellsprings which never run dry.

Not Blind but Seeing

A memorable line from Robert Burns offers a good beginning in hearing the word of Christ to us today:

"O what power the Giftie gie' us that we see ourselves as others see us . . ."

The ninth chapter of John's Gospel is about seeing, not only as others see us but seeing as God sees us. It is one of the most dramatic chapters in the New Testament, as the Savior calls out to us not to be blind, but seeing.

Trying To See What Can't Be Seen

It all begins with a question to Jesus from the disciples as they saw a man who had been born blind.

"Who sinned," they asked, "this man or his parents?" It's the kind of question we can understand. One predictable emotion in parents who are told that their newborn has a calamitous affliction such as blindness is the haunting sense of guilt. We humans instinctively search for the reasons why things happen — particularly tragic things. In the Old Testament we do learn that the sins of the fathers are visited upon the children to the third and fourth generation of those that hate him (Deuteronomy 5:9), but that is not God's vindictiveness. If a mother abuses her body during pregnancy with drug dependency, the newborn child may indeed be afflicted. But that is not to be laid at the door of the Creator. Part of our human blindness, which is a phrase meaning our sinful condition, is that we try to see cause and effect in ways we cannot see. This question on the part of the disciples is an example.

Jesus is absolutely clear in his reply. It is not that this man or his parents sinned, he says. This tragedy of blindness is to become an occasion for the manifesting of the work of God. Thus Jesus turns away the question and puts everything on a new basis entirely. We who can see only through a glass darkly (1 Corinthians 13:12) cannot fathom mysteries which God alone can probe. God acts in the face of mystery and tragedy. That is the point. Each of us needs that assurance from the Lord. We have it here on Jesus' own authority. It is futile and misleading to try to make God out as a God of retaliation. He is the God of judgment, yes. But that judgment leads to redeeming love and merciful entering into our insoluble problems of life. The rest of John 9 is all about that!

Seeing In a World Still Blind

The blind man is healed. Jesus makes clay spittle, puts it on the blind man's eyes, sends him to the Pool of Siloam in Jerusalem and tells him to wash. As he does so, "he came back seeing." (v. 7) The one who was blind from birth, who never saw color, form, motion, sky, earth, faces, who never saw the sun rise or set over his native Jerusalem, who never looked out over the walls to the loveliness of the Mount of Olives, or to the east to see the deep reddish hue of the hills of Moab in the late afternoon sun — this man was given sight by the Son of God who is the light of the world.

What should now follow? Surely this. Let the people around him rejoice with him as he sings and dances with ecstatic joy. Let his family join him and his neighbors, too, in the unending praise of Jesus who brings sight. Let the people who had the care of souls open the temple doors and shout thanksgiving and praise of God for the wondrous sign and miracle that had taken place. Let the whole town rejoice!

None of that follows.

First the neighbors begin to doubt whether this man now able to see is really the same one who was blind all those years. To them the man says, "I am the man!"

Then he is brought to the Pharisees, who denounce it all because Jesus healed the blind man on the Sabbath. A division occurs among them, some advocating affirmation, but others claiming the healer is not from God because he healed on the day of rest.

Then the man's parents are brought onto the scene; they are asked questions which can put them at odds with the Pharisees. The blindness is caused by fear. He is our son, they say. Yes, he was blind. But now — ask him for all the rest — we're not talking about it anymore. How often that has been repeated! Fear works like cataracts; it blurs and blinds and silences us when it comes to the moment for testimony.

Then it is back to the Pharisees for a second round. They are now telling the blind man what to see, and whom to see. In full hostility against Jesus, they tell the formerly blind man to praise God but to denounce this so-called prophet. By their words, Jesus is an impostor and a sinner. But now the blind man who can now truly see begins to reveal what it means to see. He taunts them with his witness that Jesus has opened his eyes to see, yet the Pharisees are refusing to honor the deed that has been done in the open sight of all! Or, he goes on, do you perhaps secretly want to become Jesus' disciple, too! At that the lid goes off. The Pharisees explode in full denunciation, not only of Jesus but of this man who had received the gift of sight. "You are born in utter sin, and would you now teach us?" They then put him out of the temple.

Finally the man is found by Jesus, who had heard of his being thrown out. Jesus asks him concerning his faith. The man is frank to say he doesn't really know who the Son of man is. "I am he," Jesus says. The man's answer is, "Lord, I believe," and he is on his knees in worship.

The man released from blindness into the world learns about a blindness that still afflicts those who can see. That is the point of the narrative the Gospel writer gives us in detail. Who is blind? Who can see? Blindness is not only a matter of sightless eyes. It is the problem of a heart and soul darkened by sin. God would not leave us in that blindness of soul that leaves us unable to see him or follow his life. Christ Jesus is God's gift of light to our world, and to all within us that obscures the brightness of the Father's image and the fullness of his life. In this light of grace, Jesus went to the Cross. His gift of himself is the great work of God that means "the eyes of our heart are opened to the hope to which God has called us." (Ephesians 1:18) God be thanked for our eyes which see. God be eternally thanked for the vision which is ours by faith that puts us alongside this bewildered man so long ago who said, "Lord, I believe."

Not Blind but Seeing: The Full Stature of Christ

As we live under Christ and his Gospel, surely we can be aware of our vision of him and the fullness of his grace as a growing vision. See Christ and the sufficiency of his Cross as his work which is established at the center of life, not on the sidelines. Religion can be a peripheral matter, having to do with ceremonial occasions such as marriage, funerals, Christmas and Easter. To see Christ as the one who gives us life and grace is never to live as though our Lord Jesus was a marginal figure in our life. Let no blindness obscure him from the center of our decisions and priorities day by day. See him at work in the heart of the world's events. Trace his Spirit's presence in the things which are foremost in your energies and activities.

Our blindness to the fullness of this stature can sometimes take the form of wrapping him in our nation's flag, as if his chief function was to sanction our enterprises as a people. Jesus can be made into an endorsement of our denomination over some other one; but that is the blindness of turning him into a cheerleader instead of Savior and Judge. It is common to want his gifts but not his people, to profess a private kind of line to him but never to see our place in the church to which he always calls us. Jesus does not go out of style. His word of truth holds for this time and every time. The blind spots in our faith life need clearing up; for that purpose he gives us a text like this one today. As long as we live, and worship, and participate in his mission, and take our place among his people, our spiritual vision will keep growing. When we come to behold him in heaven, face to face, he will be no stranger to us, nor us to him. It is his face we have been seeing all along, even among the least of his brothers and sisters. Then we shall see, no longer through a glass darkly, the gracious Lord who has been at work in our lives from the beginning.

Not Blind but Seeing: The View of Other People

To see with the new eyes of faith means to see other people with the eyes of Christ himself. People are not seen as a threat with whom we must compete and over whom we must gain control. People are not seen as problems from whom we prefer escape. People, viewed in the light of Christ, are to be seen as fellow humans whom God loves no less than ourselves. People are to be listened to, spoken to, cared about, learned from, and appreciated as channels through whom God addresses us.

When it comes to old tensions and long standing biases which divide us humans, we Christians have a calling to see people not just as stereotypes of the old problems. Being forgiven, we are called to locate those new points of beginnning in relationships that looked hopelessly mired in prejudice, jealousy, and vengeance. Conciliatory healing gets started as people *see*, with humility and penitence, what each has done to break it all off. Such seeing leads to healing, and all over our world today that kind of seeing and healing is essential!

Seeing others in faith means admonition, too. When faithless, destructive behavior takes place, we are not called to blindness which takes the form of a shrug of the shoulders and the thought that everybody does that now-a-days. Seeing sin means calling it for what it is, and seeing clearly the consequences before those consequences are not so far gone that everything is ruined.

Not Blind but Seeing: Ourselves

To see as Christ the Lord enables us to see, is to see yourself aright. Your worth in his sight is what the cross is about. To that extent he loved you! See yourself, then, as one whose worth is not established by the opinions of others, the job or money you have, your skin color or gender, or anything else. To see yourself as a redeemed and beloved child and servant of God is to find the right base for your dignity, your confidence, and your security as a person. Being blind to this is what sets us up for all the wrong kind of self-affirmation, or the denial of the fact which is plain to everyone else — we need help!

Surely each of us knows what it means to say, "If I had only seen then what I can see now!" That can be a sentence of despair but it can also be a word of hope that we can, indeed, see now. In spite of all our natural vanity, we still become our own worst critics, and when our spiritual vision grows dim we can put ourselves so far down that we see no point in even trying at life anymore. From that blindness we are released by the Gospel of Christ. See yourself as one who has a place among his people, who rejoices in his promise, who has purpose according to his will. See the spiritual center of your life as the true center of your being, and let the priorities which you establish reflect that priority which seeks first the kingdom of God and his righteousness, convinced that all the other things fall into their rightful place.

See clearly the difference between living under Christ's reign and living a life that is fully secular.

See that no grief can come to you or those who matter in your life that our Lord has not already carried, no sorrow is ours that he had not first borne. See the strength of that towering love made manifest in the darkness of Good Friday, the love in which we can bear all things, believe all things hope all things, endure all things.

Seeing in Spite of Poor Sight

Several of our members are people with sight problems. I think of Ellen Foschinbauer in her 80s, a widow now, and no longer able to read. Though her eyesight is bad, her spiritual vision is not. She is one of those splendid witnesses to the faithful Lord, whose patience under trials and whose beautiful spirit of courage and hope is an inspiration to all who are around her.

I think now of another person of our parish family. She is not yet in her teens and yet must come to terms with a strange eye disease that has made her sight problematic. Yet in her soul the vision of faith is given in her baptism; Christ is at work in her life and I see ahead for her a lifetime of great meaning and purposefulness under God. The details are not clear just now, but she is a young Christian who believes that in her handicap "the work of God will be manifest."

. . . Was Blind but Now Can See . . .

All our seeing comes by grace, amazing grace! In that gospel song there is this line, ". . . I once was lost but now am found, was blind but now I see . . ." For that, may God be praised now and always.

Authority Through Servanthood

And as Jesus was going up to Jerusalem, he took the twelve disciples aside, and on the way he said to them, "Behold, we are going up to Jerusalem; and the Son of man will be delivered to the chief priests and scribes, and they will condemn him to death, and deliver him to the Gentiles to be mocked and scourged and crucified, and he will be raised on the third day." Then the mother of the sons of Zebedee came up to him, with her sons, and kneeling before him she asked him for something. And he said to her, "What do you want?" She said to him, "Command that these two sons of mine may sit, one at your right hand and one at your left, in your kingdom." But Jesus answered, "You do not know what you are asking. Are you able to drink the cup that I am to drink?" They said to him, "We are able." He said to them, "You will drink my cup, but to sit at my right hand and at my left is not mine to grant, but it is for those for whom it has been prepared by my Father." And when the ten heard it, they were indignant at the two brothers. But Jesus called them to him and said, "You know that the rulers of the Gentiles lord it over them and their great men exercise authority over them. It shall not be so among you; but whoever would be great among you must be your slave; even as the Son of man came not to be served but to serve, and to give his life as a ransom for many."

(Matthew 20:17-28)

The Question Of Our Time

Today's sermon is on the subject of authority, based on the text above.

It is no overstatement to say that authority is the question of our time. Wherever one looks in our world today, in family, government, business life, and the church, the conclusion seems unanimous. Authority is in a bad state of erosion. Why is this so? What can be done about a matter so vital to people in every aspect of life?

The story St. Matthew tells us in today's text speaks directly to the problem of authority, and it offers the solution to the problem. That's

39

claiming a great deal for this story which seems at first to be little more than an ambitious mother wanting preferential positions for her two sons. Much more than that is there. All who have ears to hear let us hear!

The Stereotypical Jewish Mother — in All of Us

The mother of James and John wanted Jesus to insure them the right and left hand places in his Kingdom. We all know the stereotype of the meddlesome but well-meaning Jewish mother, but it is really only natural for all parents to want the best for their children. (As St. Mark tells this same story, the request comes from the sons themselves and no mention is made of the mother. [Mark 10:35-37] Never mind the detail; the point is the same.)

The point of the request about instant places of authority is that it won't mean authority. It will mean authoritarianism, which has nothing to do with genuine, God-given authority. Immediate arrival at prestigious and status-loaded places bypasses all the things that really count. These are first and foremost, a clear sense of serving. It means capacities, competence, responsibility, perseverance, moral strength, and devotion to the truth whatever the consequences. Authoritarianism eats up all one's energies in keeping others at bay, defensive maneuvers to insure one's own power, hostility to others who appear as threats, and the need to incessantly flex one's own trappings of authority.

Without even knowing it, no doubt, Mrs. Zebedee was setting her sons up for disaster. As we look at her, however, let's recognize the "Jewish mother" in all of us. Wanting to occupy the place of authority is a mightily seductive force.

I learned something about that at the tender age of nine. As a fourth grader I had a marvelous teacher whose name was Tillie Laughlin. Her name alone is a hint of her awesome gifts as a teacher; she was no ordinary person and as long as I live I am in her debt for her gifts in teaching us the basics of the English language. Diagramming sentences was her *forte*, and she made us diagram until we could see subject/predicate, noun/verb, and prepositional phrases in our sleep. (I envision her now, wincing, at our national pasttime of misusing the adverb "hopefully"!) One day in class she let me be the teacher for two minutes. There I stood, where she always stood. I could ask the whole class a question and see the hands shoot up. Then *I* could choose who would answer. It was dazzling for me to be able to choose from all those hands. I thought that was what being a teacher was mainly about, and it was a delicious sense of power that had suddenly seeped into my nine-year-old mind. But what was happening to me had nothing to do with being a teacher, and everything to do with enjoying ordering others around. This is why I can appreciate Mrs. Zebedee's eagerness to get her boys in the front seats ahead of anyone else. With a little effort and imagination, you can see the same thing in your own life.

Still to Be Seen in Our Time and Life

Jesus was talking about the rancid fruit of misplaced authority in his response to the Zebedee family, mother and sons alike.

. . . if you know that the rulers of the Gentiles lord it over them and their great ones exercise authority . . . it shall not be so among you.

(vv. 24-26)

Every day in our world, people are frustrated and brutalized by authoritarian muscle-flexing. Businesses fail. Families flounder. Armies collide. Hatreds simmer. Over and over again the sad spectacle recurs, one person seeking to dominate the other. Or one group gaining leverage over the other.

One reaction to that is despair over all authority. Being victimized by authoritarianism, people give up on everything that even looks like authority in its rightful form. Then things go from bad to worse. The world can't get along from day to day with no authority whatsoever; things won't work at all. Anarchy is no solution; rather it is a compounding of the problem. Listen carefully and look thoughtfully to yourself if you are ever told by intelligent people that they see you resisting "authority figures." The words may be more true than you want to recognize. This is not to say that all authority figures are legitimate and must be accepted without question. Ferdinand Marcos was an authority figure in the Philippines whose ouster was a work of God. Tyranny is an offense to God, whose will is for liberation in the fullest sense of the word. But that liberation he brings about does not destroy authority. It makes us free to recognize it, welcome it, and when it comes to us, use it in the right way for the good of all.

The Authority of the Servant

"He who would be great among you must be your servant, and whoever would be first among you must be your slave."

Thus Jesus turns authoritarianism on its head, and points to the rightful blessing of authority. Servant, slave are the big words here. I realize that some of us can barely stand those words. I have had people tell me to my face not to even speak these words, so sure they are that servanthood means docile, submissive, capitulation to some great evil that has been suffocating their lives for a long time. I ask you to hear me when I say that servanthood is not capitulation, nor being a slave, a docile handing of one's life over to forces which grind it to pieces.

When speaking of greatness and servanthood, being first and being slave, Jesus made the real point in one of the greatest words we have from him:

. . . even as the Son of man came not to be served but to serve, and to give his life as a ransom for many . . .

Being a servant was not giving in to evil by laying aside all he came to accomplish. Being a servant was for Jesus the fulfillment of all he came to do. He accepted denial and mockery, scourging and crucifixion, in order that he might bear up on his own shoulders the weight that the sins of the world create. He is the suffering servant, portrayed in Isaiah 53: "upon him was the chastisement that made us whole, and by his stripes we are healed." Our Lord destroyed the power of sin by bearing our sins, in his body, on the tree. That is servanthood. There is nothing docile or weak about it. It is the revelation of the strong grace of God that sin is forgiven at such an unimaginably great price as the innocent one who suffered for us.

Why We Love God and Serve Him

This Gospel I hand on to you. I am called to be a servant of this Christ. The reason why I love him and count it my highest good to serve him is because of what he has first done for me. Without that serving of my deepest needs, my life would still be caught fast in the wrong kind of authority. Isn't that true of you as well? Can't each of us make this confession, freely and from our hearts? Jesus Christ is the authority in our lives because of his servanthood. We love him, follow him, obey him, and give our lives to his service because his love has a home in our hearts.

Authority is a magnificent thing to see at work in daily life. When it arises from the Gospel and the indwelling Spirit of Christ it is never forced. We readily accord such people the authority that comes from their serving, and is necessary for their serving.

The Call to Young Christians

Young Christians, regard highly the authority of parents who love you sincerely. This is no claim to their being sinless, for they are not. But freely honor their authority as those who are over you and responsible for you in the Lord. Obedience to them is not burdensome. It can come freely, for they bear a responsibility for you and must think, act, and take care for the things that lead to your growth and happiness. Parents, accept your authority as those who serve your family with reverence for God who makes you his representatives. This calls for faith, prayers, strength in holding your convictions, and love in carrying them out for the good of your children. In an age of wholesale parental abdication of authority, your calling is to fill the vacuum. The day will come when your children will rise up and bless you.

The Call to the Whole Church

In the life of the church, authority is a great gift of the Spirit of Christ who alone is Lord among all who bear his name. The past year or two have been a nightmare of lies, accusations, covering up and general tantrums among the celebrity television evangelists whose names you know well enough from the day by day news. What happens to the authority of a public ministry when it has no moral substance? It is gone, and great numbers of people are betrayed. You have every right to look to your pastors for honesty about sin, sincere confession of it, and a firm grasp of the Gospel in making new beginnings day by day. In these times of pain for the whole church, let me tell you of a minister whose authority remains rock-solid because of her continuing servanthood.

A Radiant Servant, with Authority

I think of a woman whose ministry is concentrated on the people dying of AIDS in our city. She is quiet in her manner, but fearless in her daily rounds of prayer, counsel, medical help, and spiritual support for men and women (and now children) who have this irreversible disease destroying their lives. She has an authority because her mind is Christlike and her life is not cheapened by plastic images of great numbers, great wealth, great power in ministry. She washes the feet of the suffering day in and day out. I know her and honor her as a person of great authority. She works hard at honing her skills, and keeps growing in the competence required to minister effectively to people at the far edge of our society. Servanthood is not settling for the least in dedication. She is in earnest about her calling, and I see that depth in her spirituality most Friday mornings as she participates in a clergy group who meet regularly for prayer and study of the biblical texts we are all preaching. There is a certain beauty about her authority. It is so freely received by her, and freely given. Everything she possesses in the qualities of her mind and spirit go into the faithful giving of ministry to those she serves. Few know her. She has no great public status. Her field is uncrowded! She will never run a television ministry empire. Hers is the mind of Christ, and therein lies her authority. I listen to her with respect, and learn from her more than she knows.

Our world is constantly cockeyed in its rush to the places of honor, assuming that just being there equals authority. What the world needs is a voice, not when it thinks it is right but when it is wrong. Our God calls us to have the mind of Christ, who came not to be served but to serve — to the giving of his life. In responding to that call, he grants us an authority that is a lasting blessing. Use it well.

The Resurrection of the Body

I am the Resurrection and the life; he who believes in me, though he die, yet shall he live.

(John 11:25)

An Unsurpassed Word of Comfort

Without question, these words of our Lord are unsurpassed in the comfort, assurance, and strength they bring to all who hear them in faith. To know that the blank, the ache, and the emptiness which death brings have been met and conquered by one who is equal to the task is the best news we can ever receive. If you know what it means to listen for a footstep that never comes, to long for a voice that is no more heard, then you can cherish all the more this word of Jesus Christ which is so majestic and unfathomable. Each time we speak the Apostles' Creed we conclude with this dozen-word phrase that spans all eternity in its meaning: ". . . the resurrection of the dead and the life of the world to come." Today is a good day to see that conviction in the light of the words Jesus spoke. Here is the central thought of the sermon to guide us: God's faithfulness in raising Jesus Christ from the dead is the one basis on which we hope for life after death.

As Jesus Dealt with Grief

The occasion on which Christ spoke these words provides the necessary background for understanding their fuller meaning. In the town of Bethany, a few miles from Jerusalem, lived two sisters and a brother who opened their door and their hearts to Jesus on many a happy occasion. The man of this household, Lazarus, and died. His two sisters, Mary and Martha,

45

sent word to Jesus of his death. The news affected Jesus visibly. The word of Lazarus' death, the sound of the women weeping, and the knowledge of Lazarus' departure caused Jesus to weep openly. The simple phrase in John 2, "Jesus wept" is a powerful reminder to us of how completely our Lord shared our human nature. And, incidentally, since he had no hesitancy in expressing his deeply-felt emotions in this time of grief, we need not hold back our own tears. When Martha learned that Jesus was coming near their household in Bethany, she could not restrain herself. Hurrying forth from the door to meet him, she shows the strength of mind and faith in her earnest word addressed to Jesus:

> Lord, if you had been here, my brother would not have died. And even now I know that whatever you ask from God, God will give you.

Just what did Martha mean? Who knows? It is most likely that Martha herself did not know exactly what she meant. The hour of bereavement is an hour when we humans do not know what to think or how to express ourselves to God or man. We are numb, bleak, and chilled in the face of death. But Jesus knew all this. He did not chide Martha because her thoughts were blurred, wistful, and sad. He said, "Your brother will rise again."

The Attention Is Upon Christ, Not Lazarus

It is of the first importance that we recognize that Jesus said nothing more, nothing less, about Lazarus as he spoke to Martha. This was enough for Martha to know, that the Lord himself gave his word that Lazarus would rise. But when it comes to the question by whose power such a thing should happen, Jesus reveals the working of God the Father in his own life. "I am the resurrection and the life; he who believes in me, though he die, yet shall he live."

There is a very deliberate placement of emphasis here, one which may escape our notice if we do not take care in heeding the passage. Jesus draws the attention away from any questions about the everlastingness of life, the immortality of the soul, etc. He does not deliver well-turned phrases about the qualities of the human personality that are so powerful and unique that they cannot die and must survive. The attention is not upon humans, not even his very close friend, Lazarus. The Bible and the Creed do not speak at all of the immortal qualities of men. The attention is upon the life-giving power of God. "I am the resurrection and the life" is a truth that is worlds away from the common human assumption, "something of the best in each of us lives on . . ." If that difference is clear to you, then you are in a very good position to appreciate the decisive, revolutionary character of this word of Jesus concerning himself as the resurrection.

The Stone of Offense

The word, "I am the resurrection and the life" upon Jesus' lips means not only that he is given the power to rise again from death to life. It means that in his own victory over death, Jesus displays God's faithfulness in promising resurrection and life to all who accept his gracious work of rescuing the whole world from eternal death. Everything hinges on God's work in Jesus Christ. The Christian hope for the resurrection — rests on God's power to create and recreate anew through the atoning work of his Son. Our eternal destiny is not determined by anything innate within us, as though the life of the world to come were an automatic possession of ours simply because we share in the life that now is. According to this word of Jesus and the echo of it in the concluding phrase of the Apostles' Creed, Christ's own resurrection is the key to our present hope and our future condition. The God and sovereign Lord whom Jesus reveals is God of the living and not of the dead. (Matthew 22:31-32) It is God's quality, not man's, which guarantees the life of the world to come. This is the stumbling block over which unbelief trips and falls. It does seem absurd that everything in this life and whatever life to come is determined by the death and resurrection of Christ Jesus. But that is the Gospel. That is the same truth that meets us in every other facet of the whole truth of God. What makes it offensive to us is that we may take no credit for such an eternally precious gift. The old sinful nature that still rampages through us reacts against the supremacy of God's grace in our total life of faith before him through Jesus Christ.

Where Sin Presses Hardest on Us

Here is where sin presses hardest upon us, when we must turn our loved ones over to God through death. Indeed, the real testing is when we must ourselves face death and pass from everything in this life. No wonder, then, that St. Paul calls death the last hurdle the Spirit must lead us over before our life with God can be completed in resurrection glory!

It is an altogether natural thing to fear death. We know nothing of what lies on the other side of death. Peer as we may, our eyes can make out nothing but a veil. And so the reality of death is one we face with a shudder. All the sweet poems and lovely lyrics about the memories of loved ones withstanding, there is an unmistakable horror, loneliness, and deep sadness that grips us in the face of death. The Psalmist put his finger on the heart of it:

As for man, his days are like grass; he flourishes like a flower of the field;
for the wind passes over it, and it is gone, and its place knows it no more.

(Psalm 103:15-16)

The last phrase of this passage is the reminder that the horror of death lies in the fact of lostness, that one's life may be swallowed up by death and then forgotten by others. All that we hold dear, all that we strive for and give ourselves to disappears like a rock sinking out of sight in deep, dark water that closes over it and never leaves a trace of its path. I have often thought of this when speaking with bereaved families. In more instances than you might imagine, younger family members do not know the first names of the fathers and mothers of aged persons who have died. And so this thought comes to me, that on some evening many years hence, when my son has died and a pastor has come to comfort his own children and prepare for his funeral service, the pastor might ask, "And what was his father's name?" And no one will remember. If that might not be the case with your grandchildren and mine, it will almost surely be the case with your great-grandchildren. The point of this that is hard on us has nothing to do with the mere fact that a name is not rememberd. The poignant fact lies in this: my whole existence passes away, "and its place knows it no more." What a nameless multitude lies in dust beneath the earth! What a host of dreams and hopes have slipped into oblivion, not because of any deliberate neglect, but because death's grip is so relentless! The bravest human expressions of immortality have never been written when facing a corpse. Unless an undertaker labors long and hard in his craft over me, even my dearest loved ones cannot bear to look at my remains once death has come. Such is the devastation that sin causes as we face the fact of death.

When Benefits May Become Detours

In our day and culture, when so many remarkable gifts of God are at hand to enrich and prolong our life, we may find it harder and harder to come to terms with death. Do not misunderstand me, I do not pass judgment on miracle drugs, oxygen machines, heart resuscitators, and other medical means of extending life. But where the judgment does fall upon us is when we put such gifts of God into the place of God and think that somehow or other we are not going to have to face the fact of death. You may know the word "cryogenics" — the process of freezing a body immediately after clinical death and storing the body at liquid nitrogen temperature (-320 degrees F) without deterioration for an indefinite period. Then, the assumption goes, at some much later time ways will have been found to thaw the body without damage and to cure the cause of death. Before we all dismiss this as nonsense, we may take note of serious scientific attention to this process. If the motive to extend life is to extend one's service to fellow humans to the glory of God, then at least the motive is beyond reproach. And, remember, we live in a day when we not only sing love songs under the moon, but we send machines onto the moon! No one among us has any accurate idea of what space travel is going to mean for the question

of longevity of life and the measuring of life by time as we presently understand it. But be this all as it may, the final issue must be faced. Death cannot be indefinitely postponed. Sooner or later it comes to every door.

The Present Power of the Resurrection Hope

The Christian faith is based upon the truth that God has overcome death,
for we worship a resurrected Lord! Each time we receive Holy Communion, we join together with the whole company of faithful, both on earth
and in heaven, in praising God for his victory over death in raising his Son.
Each time we offer prayer, sing a hymn, or simply direct our minds to the
living God and his mercies, we are directing our worship to him who is the
resurrection and the life. This is what the Christian rejoices in and hopes
for: Christ's own work of conquering death. He will not abandon us in our
hour of greatest need! How could he? The very reason why he endured the
full horror of death and was raised victorious over it, was in order to dis-
close God's faithfulness to all. Put your hope in him. We do not need other
human props or detours. We look to Jesus Christ. He is with us in death
as well as life. That is all we need to know!

This sure conviction exercises a definite influence upon our whole view
of our lives here and now. When you and I know by faith that God has
a plan to raise our mortal bodies from the dust in the resurrection of all
people, we cannot treat our bodies carelessly here and now. We are for our
bodies, we treat them with honor. We recognize them as the temples of the
Holy Spirit. This is why Christians provide the benevolent ministries of hospitals, clinics, homes for the aged, care for the homeless. God has made our
bodies and redeemed them through his Son: we cannot do anything else but
honor his work as we take care for the material, physical needs of all. This
same resurrection hope is the motive for the Christian ethic. Sexual morali-
ty, for instance, is part of the Christian's way of life because we know that
the body is not a toy to be consumed by lust, but a work of honor to be
highly regarded and truly respected. It is nonsense to despise the Christian
hope as a way of escaping the present responsibilities of caring for the urgent needs of people. That is a misuse of the true biblical meaning of the
resurrection hope. God has treated our physical creation with infinite care
from the start to the eternal future of our lives. He sent his own Son in
the flesh for our sakes. That prompts the Christian to care now, because
all things are brought to glorious fulfillment in the resurrection.

What Lies Ahead

When death parts us from those we love, we must have the assurance
that only God can give, that he keeps faith with all who sleep in the dust.

Have you ever thought of this — that the finest tribute you can pay to the risen Lord is to entrust your loved ones to his unfailing care? To whom else would we want to entrust them? To whom else would we ourselves go in our last hour? We can honor our Lord in no finer way than by leaving our loved ones with him. He brings healing for our heartaches with the assurance he expresses in this text: "he that believes in me, though he die, yet shall he live . . ." The blessed dead enjoy the peaceful rest that Jesus Christ provides. They await his call to resurrection and eternal life in the glorious body he shall recreate, when he comes in glory at the end of time.

We have this hope because the Son of God has certified it by his own resurrection. We have it through his grace. This hope is his gift. Our eternal future is not decided because of our heredity or our environment. It is decided by the events which we rehearse in the Creed each Sunday. Our eternal future is determined by God's mighty deeds of love accomplished on our behalf.

This is, in effect, an Easter sermon, preached at the mid-point of Lent. It is good to preach the Easter message on this Sunday. For every Sunday is a little Easter day. Furthermore, I may not be here on earth a month from today when we celebrate the Easter victory on the Festival of the Resurrection. You may not be here, either. And so we take to heart now the great meaning of the concluding phrase of the creed, "I believe in the resurrection of the body and the life everlasting." We can say that from our hearts because of him who is the Resurrection and the Life. God's faithfulness in raising Jesus Christ from the dead is the one basis on which our hope for resurrection and eternal life rests. These words from the book of Revelation are a suitable closing for us now:

> Behold, the dwelling of God is with men. He will dwell with them, and they shall be his people. And God himself will be with them. He will wipe away every tear from their eyes, and death shall be no more, neither shall there be mourning nor crying nor pain any more, for the former things have passed away.
>
> (Revelation 21:3-4)

A Sermon
for Passion Sunday

On this Passion Sunday, we stand again at the threshold of the Great Seven Days, this week of time that takes us to the inmost heart of the work that God has done for us through Christ his Son. As we prepare to hear the passion story of Jesus' suffering as proclaimed by St. Matthew, I invite you to hear one sentence in particular. It is that word of our Lord from the Cross that is at once the most anguished account and the Gospel which comes to us from it: *"My God, my God, why hast thou forsaken me?"* (Matthew 27:46)

This word seems to be that utterance of Christ which we are most ready to understand and identify with. We can admire and worship the man who in the agony of crucifixion says, "Father forgive them, for they know not what they do." Likewise, for the second and third words he speaks — what else but wondering praise and adoration can we offer to the man who promises paradise to a pentitent thief and who commends his mother to the care of a faithful disciple as he leaves this world? As we realize the infinite power and love of God's Son that enabled him to pray for his tormentors in his mortal hour we must worship and admire from a distance because we know that nothing in us is capable of that selfless reaction to suffering. But the man who in pain cries out with a loud voice, "My God, why hast thou forsaken me?" is heart of my heart and mind of my mind. He has entered the darkest mystery of human life, the mystery of defeated goodness and victorious evil. Listening to this word, we recognize one who said what we would have said as our first and last and only word from a cross. Yes, this word draws us to Christ not because of his divinity, but rather because of his humanity. This is no word of suffering nobility and heroic detachment from his agony. This is the word which tells us he shared the tragedy, the uncertainty, and the dark loneliness of human life to the last full measure.

51

We Have Our Own Questions of "Why?"

I do not mean to say that we can fully understand this anguished cry of our Lord. I am only wanting to remind you that in a much, much smaller measure, we all know the feeling of forsakenness. We have it whenever we feel that we have been asked to shoulder some burden that appears greater than we can bear. It happens whenever we feel that some suffering — our own or even greater, someone we love — is totally and absolutely undeserved or without rhyme or reason. Above all, it comes over us when we feel that in this place of pain God doesn't care, God offers no help, God has turned away his face and forgotten. That was what Jesus Christ felt at this moment.

We know something of what he felt, for we have felt it and asked the same anguished question. Years ago, I remember seeing a picture of the late secretary general of the United Nations, Dag Hammarskjold. His family allowed only one floral wreath to be draped across his coffin, and written across the ribbon was the single word, "Why?" How many times hasn't that word reappeared in a thousand ways, "Why did this happen to me?" A husband loses his wife, a mother loses her son, a man loses his hearing, a child loses its sight. Instinctively the question which comes to our lips is "Why?" Why should life be so unfair? Why should the world be so cold and unfeeling? Why should fate be so bitter and cruel? How easy it is, seeing Jesus Christ hanging on his Cross and hearing him speak this fourth word, to say, "See, even Christ himself was finally forced to ask why! And even Jesus went out of this life without getting the answer! What can there be in his Gospel for me?"

What This Word Reveals

But this would be a complete misreading of the words Jesus spoke. Hanging in death on his Cross, our Lord did not ask the old question in the manner we do. He did not throw out his question whether there was any purpose or reason in life, or any justice in its fate. That is the first great difference between his question and ours. When we ask why, we address the question to life or fate or the universe, almost as though we believed life were some kind of calculating machine that should invariably ring up happiness for the good and misery for the bad. In our thinking and believing, so often we make God a kind of impersonal third party, somewhere outside of our living. Thus we ask, "Why did God forsake me?" But Jesus, when drinking the bitterest dregs of his passion, did not question God as a third party, an outsider, a remote stranger. Rather, he said, "*My* God . . . why?" And that is a very different question from "Why has God forsaken me?" The former is a dialogue; the latter only a lonely and forlorn muttering to ourselves. In this hour of anguish, with his body contorted in agony and his ashen face streaked with blood, he spoke to the God whom he personally knew and personally trusted. It was not, "Why has *he*?" but "Why have *you*?" Even though he questioned the ways of the Father, failed to grasp his purpose, was unable to fathom his activity, of this one thing he was certain and of this one thing he would not let go. God was still his Father. Never did Jesus permit even the direst circumstance to make God a stranger or an enemy. The relationship between Jesus and the Father was not like our relationship to the Taj Mahal or the North Pole, something we have heard about, read about, but never known. No! Even in loneliness, lostness, and forsakeness, the cry goes up, "My God . . . why have you forsaken me?"

The Son of God Comes All the Way to Our Human Plight

And now comes the point. God is at work through the forsakenness of his Son. The purpose he achieves means rescue for nothing less than mankind, for you and for myself and for all. This Jesus who said of himself, "I and my Father are one," and "He that has seen me has seen the Father," no longer saw the Father. In place of divine intimacy, a wretched barrenness came over him. Between him and divine strength was an impenetrable, terrible wall. His prayers received no answer. His weeping received no comfort, God had no relief for his Son. God himself withdrew from his Son and precisely thereby God intervened in the death on Calvary and made it the decisive event of all time. For only by forsaking his Son does God make him like unto us in every respect. Christ completely took our place. He suffered all that *really* was ours. That meant that he had to suffer the separation from God that hung over all of us because of the rift which sin creates between God and man. The very wrath under which we stand, the very judgment pronounced upon our sins, strike him. Our punishment is laid on the innocent one. When God forsook Jesus Christ, in the words of St. Paul, "He made him to be sin for us who knew no sin." (2 Corinthians 5:21)

The Truth at Which We Wonder

We humans have found this incredible over the centuries. A little survey of the history of the interpretation of this word in Christendom during the past 2,000 years show repeated attempts to escape from the stark horror of its meaning and to flee from it. A student of the subject has listed some of the characteristic ways of getting around the sharp truth this word reveals. Some say that Jesus spoke this word for us, that he was never forsaken by God but that we were. Others say that Jesus does not pray for himself, but in place of the Jews, whom God has forsaken since they crucified Jesus. Or, the forsakenness applies only to Jesus' body. And still others contend that Jesus was only quoting Psalm 22, which begins with these words, "My God, my God, why hast thou forsaken me?" but that he was thinking of the entire Psalm which includes further words of great trust and praise.

God's Word on the Question

But all such efforts to interpret away the plain meaning of the words result in nothing more than an effort to abandon the full meaning of the Cross of Christ. God did cut off his Son in this hour, and for the most important of reasons:

> . . . since we humans have a mortal nature, Jesus also shared it, like us, in order that by his death he might dethrone the lord of death, the devil, and free from their slavery men who had always lived in fear of death . . . For it was not angels, but the descendants of Abraham that he came to help. And so he had to be made like his brothers in every respect, so that he might prove a compassionate high priest as well as one faithful in his service to God, in order to forgive the people's sins.
>
> (Hebrews 2:14-18)

One of the most helpful illustrataions on this truth I know is the one offered in the writings of the late C. S. Lewis. He likens our human situation as sinners to a box, filled with precious gems, which lies on the bottom of the sea — quite useless and far away from its intended place of usefulness and beauty. If that treasure is to be recovered, a diver must come all the way to where it is. Coming half-way or nearly all the way down into the deep, cold, dark waters will avail nothing. The diver must come all the way to where that treasure is caught fast in the mud and darkness of the deep. Thus it is with God's plan of rescue for the treasure of his human creation. His Son came all the way to where we are.

The Word of Unsurpassed Comfort

We must not miss, then, the true import of this most anguished word of pain our Savior ever spoke. This word is the most comforting to us of all! Let no one think that this word of Jesus is a relapse from his redeeming purpose, and that it would improve the record if this word could somehow be erased from the Bible. No, everything depends upon this, that the crucified one was really forsaken by God, that he came all the way to our place as offenders, and suffered the consequences we deserved. For Christ's loud lament of his forsakenness by God means to us and to the world, "You mortals, hear this: God again turns to you by his punishment for sin." By sentencing his Son to bear a burden unthinkable for us to shoulder ourselves, God lifts us up in the love of his Son. By rejecting Christ he receives us again as his own. God's forsaking of the crucified one means that he accepts the sacrifice of his Son. Therefore, since Christ was forsaken by God, there is no longer any abandonment by God. The whole family of man dies in him, and by his resurrection, all are given access to God's mercy! If you believe in Christ, that he was forsaken by God in your stead, then in him you have a communion with God that nothing can tear apart. Since Christ suffered the wrath of God, there is no longer a despair that is irremovable. Now, for us, there is no place nor moment in human experience where we can say that God cannot retrieve me, recover me, strengthen me, and nourish me with that Word of his which he spoke after his passion and resurrection, "Lo, I am with you always, even unto the end of the world." That is no cheap, idly offered word. Before he could say that word to us, he first had to say, "Why hast thou forsaken me?" There is no comfort, either in the Old or New Testament, that does not have its ultimate foundation in this cry of agony. This word, so filled with the hardest pangs of suffering, has become the welcome word of our victorious brother and Lord through his resurrection from the dead.

Therefore Keep Christ Jesus in Life's Center

I am not wanting to say that any ordeal is something to relish or look forward to, or that distress and suffering are pleasant and easy to bear. What I am wanting to say is that when you and I keep Christ our Lord at the center of our lives, then we may hold fast to the truth that all our troubles can no longer be the final and ultimate suffering. Before we ever lived, he took it from us and bore it for us. Our sin is forgiven. Our loneliness is ended. Through Christ we are free to approach our Father with confidence!

The Two Washings

On this Maundy Thursday let us ponder again the Cross of Christ our Savior and its consequences for us all. One way to approach such a task as this is to direct our thinking to two washings that take place in connection with the passion of Christ.

The first one is described by the Evangelist Matthew:

> *So when Pilate saw that he was gaining nothing, but rather that a riot was beginning, he took water and washed his hands before the crowd, saying, "I am innocent of this man's blood, see to it yourselves."*
>
> (Matthew 27:24)

The First Washing

It concerns Pontius Pilate, who had declared Jesus innocent on two distinct occasions in the course of that wildly frightful early morning of our Lord's crucifixion day. But when faced with a frenzied mob, shouting not for justice but for blood, Pilate chose to side with the mob and turned Jesus over to be crucified. Having caved in to the pressure of sinful men, Pilate ordered a basin of water and made a public gesture of his avoidance of responsibility — *his* responsibility for defending an innocent man. He washed his hands in the view of the whole multitude. And then he told them that they would have to bear the guilt for what was to follow.

A Symbol We Can Recognize

We look back at this moment from the distance of all the intervening centuries, and yet its meaning is not remote at all. Surely each of us present in this worship service can recognize in the symbol of Pilate's washing his hands of Jesus a point of connection with our own experience. Among all

57

the brutal things done against Jesus in his suffering and death, this single gesture of Pilate stands out as a point at which we can identify.

As Christians intent upon being serious about our faith and our understanding of why Christ had to suffer and die, we may have a problem in identifying with the people who pressed a crown of thorns into his skull, or who whipped him, or who spit on him, jeered him . . . and finally stretched out his arms across the heavy wooden beam of the Cross and drove the spikes through his palms and wrists and ankles. That level of brutality is so overwhelmingly ugly and repulsive that we cannot honestly see ourselves doing that. Yes, our sins brought all that on. But still, we cannot grasp that fact in connection with the violence surrounding the events which literally brought on Jesus' death.

But the hand-washing gesture is something else.

Have you ever known what it means to stand face to face with a person who needed you as the one and only human being who could intervene in a threatening circumstance and prevent total chaos and disaster from occurring . . . and then sidestep that responsibility? Do you know what it is to wash your hands of another person? Is there anything in your recollection or mine that brings back to us the memory of having dismissed ourselves of care for another person in a moment of the other's genuine need? Surely each of us knows that experience.

It is not that we arranged the grand gesture of water and basin and towel before the world, to declare our innocence by such a display of imagined innocence. We have other ways, much more discreet. These include phrases such as, "Look, I really don't have time to help you right now," "Why call on me now? That's your problem," "You got yourself into this mess; you will have to get yourself out." Such phrases come to my mind, because they have come out of my mouth. I am convicted by the hand-washing symbol of Pilate, because I have missed my responsibility, failed another, walked out on a duty I should have performed when some other needed it more than I will ever know. And I take it I am not alone in this place today with such an awareness of my own soul.

The Besetting Sin of Our Times

Pilate's hand-washing gesture haunts us all, because it recurs throughout our world. It infects us in such pernicious ways in our times. I hear people speak of the "Kathy Genovese syndrome" — meaning the frightful thing of dozens of apartment dwellers doing nothing when a young women named Kathy Genovese was murdered in cold blood in the courtyard of a New York City apartment complex some year ago. That syndrome surfaces in the mindset of a person who sheds a marriage with a shrug and the comment: "I outgrew my spouse." It returns in the sin of a nation closing its doors to refugee people standing at its borders, seeking entrance in order to spare their lives and the lives of whatever families they have left. In the personal realm, in the public domain of life, that sin is repeated in countless ways day by day. It is for all of this that Jesus endured it to the death.

The spirit of avoidance of responsibility, of failure to care, of refusal to risk doing that which sustains justice and furthers love is troubling us more than we ever realize. See it in this way, however. It is not just that we fail each other. Accoding to Jesus' parable of the final judgment in Matthew 25, it is he who comes to us and knocks at the door of our lives in the persons of the suffering, the victims of injustice, the poor and castaways of the earth. Our sin is against him as well as those whom he calls his brothers and sisters.

Since that is the reality, we have our repenting to do today. It is for us that he endured it all. In his cross there is an indictment of our sin.

The Other Washing

Christ himself took a towel and basin in another moment of the passion story. St. John tells us that on the night of his betrayal, when he had gathered the twelve in the Upper Room in Jerusalem for the passover meal, this took place:

> *Jesus, knowing that the Father had given all things into his hands, and that he had come from God and was going to God, rose from supper, laid aside his garments, and girded himself with a towel.*
>
> (John 13:5)

What a remarkable verse! The Evangelist sets this simple gesture in a not-so-simple framework of divine truth. Jesus had come from God and was going to God. All things had been given to him by the Father — those are words of vast importance and a depth of meaning that we cannot fully wrap our minds around. But what we can see and grasp is the picture of the Savior with towel and basin, attending to the most humble of duties of a household servant — washing the feet of those at table.

Let this washing tell you its full truth! Let your mind and heart dwell upon the absolute contrast between this washing and that of Pontius Pilate. Here there is nothing of avoidance, of dismissal, of shameful escape and abandonment. Here the whole meaning has to do with acceptance of redeeming service, the outreach of love, the bearing of the most humble of tasks in order to accomplish the greatest of purposes.

Jesus' act of washing the disciples' feet is the symbol for his cross and the cleansing of the whole life which his atoning work at Calvary has ac-complished. He did for us what only he could do, the one who came from God and who was going to God.

This is the Gospel. Christ humbled himself for us and was obedient to the death on the cross. Our sins are foi given, no longer held against us, no longer there in God's mind and memory to stir his wrath over our colossal failures in every way. Those sad memories of occasions when we have played the part of Pilate are behind us, not ever to claim us and defeat us in the despair which the knowledge of our sins creates. All that is put away, washed clean from us. We have been served by the Son of God who loved us with a love so great and deep and pure that we can only respond with the deepest thanks of our hearts.

Not to Refuse This Washing

Peter was startled at first by the washing Jesus initiated around the circle of the disciples. And then he was offended. This turning-of-the-tables was not in order. It is Jesus who should be served by having his feet washed, and without question Peter was ready to volunteer. But Jesus set the matter straight; unless the disciples will be served by their Lord, they have no part of him. Thus the church is forever instructed to ask for mercy, to accept forgiveness, to welcome the Gospel as our one true treasure and the only power which holds us to God and to one another.

To Wash One Another's Feet

Our Lord did go on to a further word to us about this second washing we find in the passion story. "If I, then, your Lord and master, have washed your feet, you also ought to wash one another's feet. If you know these things, blessed are you if you do them."

Being washed, we have washing to do. Being served, we are called and sustained in the fulfilling work of serving people in Christ's name. The self-enclosing circle of living for the self is broken. Being loved, we have learned how to love at last. Such loving and such serving has its risks and its burdened side, but it is yet our fulfillment as Christians. For we are placed in the best of all circles of life: involvement! Involvement with him and with people in his name.

Several evenings ago I had an experience I must share with you. My wife and I drove out to a community several hours to the west of us to visit a woman and her family. She is in her mid-forties and was formerly a member of our congregation. Her husband and she moved west more than a decade ago, but we have kept in touch now and then. Just a week ago he had come by to tell me that his wife was in the final stages of a long cancer battle and would soon die. We went to minister to her. She received Communion that evening, with her family joining hands around the bedside. She spoke to us all of her confidence that Christ would see her through the last leg of the hard journey, and soon she would be in his peace and eternal care. She spoke with love and encouragement to her family members — serving them with a tremendously powerful witness to the sufficiency of the

Gospel. Her family included her sixteen-year-old daughter, who has been handling most of the cleaning, the cooking, and the shopping for the rest of the family these recent months. This splendid young girl, so quiet and unassuming in her manner, has also bathed her mother daily, and helped with all of the demanding tasks of serving a person who is dying by inches. But this daughter would not think of walking out on her mother. As hard as it is to part with one that close, the *being able to serve* is one of the chief things that makes that release possible. It is not a burden to have to serve; it is a blessing to be able to serve.

Life's greatest regret is to miss such serving, and life's foremost reward and fulfillment is to be able to serve even the least of our fellow humans in the knowledge that thus we are rendering service to Christ himself.

Two washings come to our minds this Maundy Thursday. One by Pilate the other by Christ. Two washings and two whole worlds. One of sin, the other of grace. One of death, the other of life. One of abandonment, the other of fulfillment. One of bane, the other of blessing.

Can there be any doubt about which washing blesses, comforts and strengthens us? And is there any confusion about the direction ahead for us — as those who have been washed by our servant Lord, and who are called to serve — even as he served us?

The Friday We Call Good

A Strange Title for This Day

We call this Friday — good.

I recall a comment by a person who challenged this tradition of calling the day of Jesus' crucifixion a good day. She told me that there was enough betrayal, denial, violence, bloodshed and death in the world. The idea of coming together in a church to hear of all this as it was heaped on Jesus was too much for her. She could not hear of it without coming to tears, or feeling a combination of outrage and depression.

From Other Traditions

But still we call this Friday Good Friday, as Christians in the English speaking world have done for centuries. Our Spanish speaking fellow Christians speak of this day as *Viernos Santo* — "holy Friday." The Germans speak of it as *Kar Freitag* — literally "the Friday of pure gold." Swedes know it as *Lang Fredag* — "long Friday," implying unhurried devotion throughout the day on the meaning of the Cross. From these and many other traditions come names for the day that refer to its supreme value and importance to all who believe the Gospel.

The Fruits of His Sacrifice

We call this Friday good because of its meaning. We cherish the day not because of a sordid curiosity over one man's excruciating ordeal of going through a crucifixion. It is the consequence of that great sacrifice that occupies us. Its fruits bring about our redemption. We are here in worship to behold the meaning of the cross from God's perspective.

The Witness of St. John

The account of Jesus' passion given us in St. John's Gospel is particularly well suited for this purpose. Today we hear both the eighteenth and nineteenth chapter of John in this Tenebrae service. There is a distinctive strand of emphasis running throughout these chapters, indeed throughout the entire Gospel of John. God is in charge, so to speak. In spite of the cruelty, treachery, and injustice heaped upon Jesus from every side, he is not simply a victim of circumstances. He enters into the ordeal fully, with nothing spared. But he does so with an air of mastery. He is the one who sees and knows that the Father is working out his purposes of saving love through everything that seems to oppose it.

At Each Critical Point

At the Last Supper in the upper room, Judas prepares for the act of betrayal. Our Lord says, in the presence of the betrayer and the other eleven disciples, "See, my betrayer is at hand," and puts the whole shameful deed in the context of the fulfillment of what was prophesied a millennium before in Psalm 41: "he who ate my bread lifted up his heel against me." At his arrest in the Garden of Gethsemane, Jesus intervenes against the impulsive effort of Peter to defend him with a sword. "Shall I not drink the cup my Father has given me?" he states. The he heals the one whose head was slashed by Peter's sword, thereby sparing the disciples the inevitable reprisal that would have brought them all to doom. Before the religious court of Caiaphas, the high priest that year, Jesus calmly announces to those arranging his condemnation, "You shall see the Son of man seated at the right hand of power." Before Pontius Pilate, the Roman governor of Syria who held the power to free Jesus or send him to death, Jesus said, "You would have no power over me at all unless it had been given you from above."

At every critical point, when it seems that all the wrong forces were prevailing, Jesus speaks as the one who is in control. And he is. Before Good Friday ever dawned, Jesus had said, "I am the Good Shepherd. I lay down my life for the sheep . . . no one takes my life from me. I lay it down of my own accord . . . and I take it again. This charge I have received from my Father." (John 10:11 ff)

The Cost of His Kingship

When Pilate shoved Jesus in front of the mob with the taunting slur, "Here is your king!" he did not begin to grasp the real truth of Jesus' Kingship. The regal air that dominates our Lord all through the events of his trial and crucifixion bear witness to God's power at work through his Son. As our sovereign Savior, Jesus did not soar above the bloody sweat, the pain and horror of suffering and death, but entered into it so as to take hold of it and conquer it through enduring it. He turned the wrath of humans to the purposes of God's accomplishing our salvation. Nothing takes him by surprise, nor moves him to work out a plea bargain compromise. With frenzy and fanatical hatred bursting out all around him, Jesus is strong and steady in his mission to carve out the pathway through all that our sins create. That includes death itself.

Here Is Our Center

It is here that our faith is centered. What we preach on Good Friday, and every opportunity of proclamation on every day, is Christ crucified — and risen, for us. There is no other foundation on which we can establish our trust. Religion itself can be so twisted and distorted without this lifegiving center in the Cross. When religion is misused for personal greed or simply as a cloak for control over others, the spectacle is disgusting. The worst thing is to begin to think that God is like that! But when the attention is fully and steadily upon the Cross, and Jesus as the Lamb of God who took upon himself the sins of the world at that Cross, then religion is never weird or manipulative or disgusting. It is nothing less than new life and salvation. It is the source of our faith, and the power that brings forth every fruit of faith: love, joy, peace, patience, kindness, goodness, gentleness, faithfulness, and self-control.

Not Words as Much as Silence

Today our words should be few. The power lies in silence, and the awareness that the growing darkness around us in this church has to do with the deadly power of sin and its destructiveness in us and the world. But as the lights finally go out, and we pray in total darkness, the single candle left upon the altar is briefly removed. Thus we visualize without words, in darkness, our awareness of the reason why Jesus suffered death. But the candle returns. There it still remains on the altar. In the silence of the coming moment, let that lighted candle tell you the good news. It speaks of death conquered and sin forgiven. It speaks of resurrection, of Easter, of the victory of God — at such an enormously great cost.

Times come when the spoken words of this Good Friday are not remembered. We may be too sick, too dispirited, too pressured by calamity to remember words. But let this sight stay with you. In the midst of the darkest dark, the lighted candle shines out — with its message of Christ's grace and peace.

Then we can know as never before how true it is to speak of this Friday as Good Friday.

Where Easter Begins

Now on the first day of the week Mary Magdalene came to the tomb early, while it was still dark, and saw that the stone had been taken away from the tomb. So she ran, and went to Simon Peter and the other disciple, the one whom Jesus loved, and said to them, "They have taken the Lord out of the tomb, and we do not know where they have laid him." Peter then came out with the other disciple, and they went toward the tomb. They both ran, but the other disciple outran Peter and reached the tomb first; and stooping to look in, he saw the linen cloths lying there, but he did not go in. Then Simon Peter came, following him, and he went into the tomb; he saw the linen cloths lying, and the napkin, which had been on his head, not lying with the linen cloths but rolled up in a place by itself. Then the other disciple, who reached the tomb first, also went in, and he saw and believed; for as yet they did not know the scripture, that he must rise from the dead.

(John 20:1-9)

As That Dawn Broke

As St. John's Gospel begins to tell us the greatest news that can ever come to human ears and hearts — "Christ is risen!" — there are details that puzzle us.

Mary Magdalene was the first to reach the tomb of Jesus; she arrived before the breaking of the dawn on that first day of the week. Upon finding the tomb empty she ran to tell Peter that the tomb was empty (not that Jesus was risen). Peter heard the disturbing news from Mary. He in turn ran to the grave site, accompanied by John. They looked into the tomb, John being hesitant to enter, but not Peter. They saw the burial clothes and the napkin for Jesus' head rolled up separately.

These details seem curious to us. Why are they included? What difference does it make who got to the tomb first? Does it matter that the grave clothes lie there as they do, with the napkin rolled up separately?

67

The Call to Believe

The reason for these seemingly irrelevant details is connected to the purpose John has for the hearers. It is the call to faith! Amidst the melancholy accoutrements of death and burial and the unexplained emptiness of the tomb, John is calling us to believe. Not just to believe that these desultory items of description happen to be true. The call is to believe that Jesus is the risen Christ of God.

Easter begins with all things dark, with grief and emptiness, and uncertainty everywhere. That is where Easter has to begin, because that is where the Easter Gospel meets us.

God's Own Deed

Easter really begins, of course, with the mighty work of God himself, who raised his Son from the grave at a moment and in a manner that no human eye observed. Easter begins, not with the satisfying of our curiosity as to how a dead body could begin to stir and move and stand up and push the rock away and walk out into Joseph's garden. Easter begins with the mystery and the grandeur of that deed by which the Father glorifies his Son by declaring him victor over death and all that brought him to the Cross and grave. Easter has to do with God's will to present his risen Son as the answer to our sin and our death-prone ways as people who live in a fallen world. Easter begins with God's action and grace through his Son — for the forgiveness of our sin.

Where Easter Is Needed Among Us

We all have very good reason to be deeply grateful that Easter begins where John puts that beginning, since we all have our moments when the stone seems immovable and our hopes and most earnest purposes appear to lie forever buried. It is hard for us to see fine things die: a marriage, a career, family ties, a sound business, a promising community, a church body. Our hopes are assualted when a doctor tells us as gently as he can the the suspect disease is a killer. So much of life can be lived with no reference to that empty grave in Jospeh's garden.

I think of such a person today. She is spending her twenty-fifth Easter in a hospital or nursing home. Shirley Krier is totally paralyzed by a crippling disease. Her husband left her long ago and has remarried. She has no children. Not more than a week ago someone stole the diamond out of her wedding band as she lay helpless in her bed at a nursing home. Such tragic and heartless mistreatment of one human against another lowers our hopes and makes the stone seem all the weightier that buries our aspirations for what life can be.

It can happen that way, not only when crisis situations leave us numb, but also when the life of our soul is gradually eroded by the day-to-day priorities given over to just staying alive, paying taxes, looking after ourselves, and settling into a way of life that makes a little or nothing out of the resurrection of Christ Jesus.

But Now Is Christ Risen

God is merciful beyond our imagining. In spite of our lowered hopes and minimal expectations, he still reaches out for us with redeeming love. The tomb of his Son is empty, and the stone is rolled away. The power of his resurrection victory is not lost on the world.

Where Easter Leads: Look Around You!

We can see that witness today in people all around us here in church. Just look around you. In so many faces and in so many hearts, there are so many stories of faith and spiritual strength. I have seen some of you in hard moments of crisis, and have seen you hold fast to this resurrection hope which we celebrate today. You know that Easter is still Easter when we're waiting anxiously outside an intensive care unit in a hospital, or working through a trying job problem, or mending broken fences in a tense family problem. Many of you know what it means to start out as did the women on that first Easter morning, but then discover that the tomb is empty and the unmovable stone is rolled away after all.

What I mean comes to light in a beautiful note written by one of our members to another. The woman who writes knows what it is to do battle with a chronic disease which requires constant treatment. She said to another member of the church, "Take it from me that God has been my only strength in my many ups and downs. Many times when I was alone in the dark hospital room at night, if it wasn't for my belief that God was always with me, I'd have been lost." It is to that kind of persistent, durable courage for coping with a lifelong problem that Easter leads.

Where Easter Leads: Listen to Its Sounds

We can hear that witness today, sung by children, youth, and adult choirs and accompanied by all the instruments which thrill our souls. How much these gifted and faithful people do for us! So many people of all ages are experiencing the excitement of worship. They want to be here. They look forward to taking part. They work hard to prepare for this day, and its memory will return to bless them in coming years of worship and active serving in congregations. That's where Easter leads!

Where Easter Leads at Last

Where Easter leads, at last, is to that glorious presence of the risen Christ who shall at the great and final day raise our bodies and present us to God for life eternal. Today is a foretaste of that final glory. Possessing the resurrection hope makes a difference in our dying as well as our living. Among other things which describe that difference is this: we can laugh in the face of death. Not a nervous, silly laughter, which betrays a deeper uneasiness or dread of death, not a gallows humor which reveals a cynicism about death. But a laughter that has a genuine ring to it, a laughter that reveals a trust that since Christ the Lord has conquered death, we might as well enjoy his victory with an ease of heart and spirit that includes a sanctified sense of humor.

A Sound the Devil Cannot Bear

A friend of mine, Robert Herhold, is a west coast pastor whose brother died some time ago. Listen to his description of the ministry that went on between brothers in the final days before his brothers death:

> My brother experienced eternal life before he died. Eternity began in time for him. We laughed and kidded up to his last day in the hospital where he was also the administrator. I thought I was ministering to Wayne, but I discovered that he was ministering to me. We prayed often and in one of our last prayers, he thanked God for our being together . . . God seemed to draw him closer and closer to himself, but strangely not further from us. When I would get overly religious, Wayne would puncture it with his humor. He once awoke and asked if he had said anything incriminating in his sleep. I assured him that he had. "How much did I pledge to the church?" he inquired! . . . In those last days — not last but beginning days — Wayne moved gracefully from the things on earth to the things above. His humor became sharper as his perspective deepened. He suffered awhile longer, stayed around long enough to let us know, without words, that we need not fear nor sorrow overmuch because he knew the Lord who would not let go.

That, finally, is where Easter leads: to the ringing, joyous, hearty, jubilant laughter and singing and celebrating of that glorious company of heaven who surround the risen Lord and sit at his table.

Let Him Lead You to This Goal

God is ever trying to give us hints of eternity, sending us so many faithful men and women whose lives are hid with Christ in God. He is trying in every way he can to show us where Easter begins, where it leads, and finally what its ultimate goal is. And, particularly, he sends us his Son who gives us the forgiveness of sin and the victory over grace. Christ is seated at the right hand of God in glory, and yet is also present with us now in the Gospel which we proclaim in word and sacrament:

At the Lamb's high feast we sing
Praise to our victorious King,
Who has washed us in the tide
Flowing from his pierced side. Hallelujah!

Praise we him whose love divine
Gives his sacred blood for wine
Gives his body for the feast
Christ the victim, Christ the priest. Hallelujah!

Believing Is Seeing

And Jesus said to him, "Thomas, do you believe because you have seen me?
Blessed are those who have not seen and yet believe."

(John 20:29)

Seeing is believing, we commonly say.

But this text turns it around. Believing is seeing. On that memorable evening in Jerusalem, following the Lord's resurrection by eight days, he appeared to the eleven disciples once again — this time with Thomas present. Remember how he invited Thomas to touch his wounded hands and side, and then spoke the words we hear on this second Sunday of Easter so many centuries later, "Blessed are those who have not seen and yet believe."

With that declaration, Jesus sets aside once and for all the thought that we are somehow at a disadvantage in comparison with those who saw his resurrected body. Thomas had wanted to verify everything by sight and touch. "Unless I see his hands . . . and put my finger into the nailprints, I will not believe . . ." That sentence has been repeated in so many various ways down through the ages since. But Jesus does not link his resurrection presence to those who could see and touch him. The priority lies with faith.

How do we come to faith, and stay strong in faith?

Faith comes by hearing, St. Paul says in a celebrated passage from Romans 10, which is timely for us to hear in connection with the Gospel reading for this day:

> *. . . whoever calls on the name of the Lord will be saved. But how shall*
> *they call on him in whom they have not believed? And how shall they be-*
> *lieve in him of whom they have not heard? And how shall they preach un-*
> *less they are sent . . . so then faith comes by hearing, and hearing by the*
> *word of God.*
>
> (Romans 10:14-18)

This is how we have been brought to faith: by hearing the Word of the crucified and risen Lord. What a great mystery and marvel that is. God's

73

Spirit is pleased to draw us to Christ by something as apparently inconsequential as a spoken message. Yet God puts all his redeeming love and purpose for us into a word that can be spoken, a word that comes to us in our words, joined with water in Baptism and with the bread and wine of the Eucharist. We do not believe on our own and of ourselves; if so our faith would forever be dependent upon our own power. Our trust and assent that Jesus is Lord comes from the hearing of the Gospel.

Believing the resurrected Lord is risen for the remission of our sins, you and I are given sight to behold what can take place in our world — things we would never see without the undergirding of faith.

This came home to me strongly some time ago when I wish you could have been with me for an evening with several hundred of Chicago's lay Christian leaders. Senator Mark Hatfield was speaking. He portrayed much of what he sees as a "late afternoon" mood among our people — tired out and worn down by seemingly intractable problems of economy, moral compromise, and the threat of nuclear holocaust. Then he began to really take hold of the problems as one who believes in Christ's resurrection and therefore sees what divine providence tells us to hope for and to do. Citing generous portions of the prophet Jeremiah, and even more abundant reference to our Lord's decisive victory over all the principalities and powers by his resurrection, Hatfield challenged us all to do away with mindless consumerism in the better interests of responsible stewardship of the earth. With the Easter hope as his ground, he gave us reasons to hope that under God we can find our security not in multiplying nuclear warheads but in strengthening the moral fabric of our personal and public life. Knowing what Senator Hatfield has done in the U.S. Senate in Washington D.C., and knowing something of what he does among the unemployed people in his home state of Oregon's forestry industry, I am mightily impressed with the vision of a Christian man in public office who sees much because he believes the essentials of the biblical truth about God's judgment upon sin and his grace for sinners.

He gives us an example to follow. His witness is a powerful and relevant commentary on this text.

During the past week some of us have been rejoicing in blessings, others groaning under burdens. Whatever the case, this Sunday has nothing to do with post-Easter letdown. The very thought of it is totally out of order. Instead it has everything to do with believing the Easter texts, and seeing the Easter faces of people with whom we serve out our calling.

Texts and faces. Take both to heart as we think of our part in the great purposes the risen Lord is accomplishing through his church in our world.

In the church we have texts. We live by the word of the living God. Think how many people in the ages since the first Easter have heard this text: "blessed are those who have not seen and yet believe." In times of famine and war, under circumstances of persecution and exile, amidst all the perplexities which beset men and women and youth, the Easter word has been spoken and heard in faith. We do not have mere reports and analyses; we have texts — the sure and abiding word of the living God that he can and does act in the middle of terrible problems for the rescue and helping of people everywhere. Such a word proclaims "a faith that overcomes the world." (1 John 5:4) We live in the middle of such strong temptations to give in to the world, to live by the secularity that undermines the resurrection of Christ as the only sure foundation. Equally forceful are the currents that would incline us to escape from the world. But God calls us to live in the faith which overcomes the world. The Scripture underlies that faith. We have texts. And so, if today finds you concerned by anxieties or worn down by a late afternoon sense of how futile it is to even try to believe anymore, listen to the text. That text has strengthened and renewed the hearts of many like yours before.

Believing the text gives us the vision of faith to see faces. From whatever vantage point one begins to understand what we're up against in today's world, there are always reams of statistics and endless generalizations that point to a depressed economy, a self-serving spirit of narcissism, and mounting numbers of marriages and families that have been shipwrecked. But we must still see faces. It is faces of people in job application lines that we must recognize — each one a person with a dignity and destiny under God. In what is popularly termed the "Me Generation," we still must discern faces of people who are trying — some wrongly and others faithfully — to make sense out of life. We must not know Communists as a faceless multitude far away to the east; we must look for faces — including those faces this very day in the Soviet Union who celebrate Easter amidst totalitarian forces which would quench social disease. We must see faces — those of men and women and young people who are caught and struggling with a monstrous problem of life. Faces. The church must always have an eye for faces, for people — believing each one to be made in the Father's image and forever the object of the Father's searching love.

In the late afternoon of his own ministry, Jesus once encountered a distraught father who had reached the end of his rope with a violent son whose convulsive and terrifying behavior had driven everyone to despair. The momentous story, tied so directly to our times with scores of thousands of young people escaping into the swampland of drug abuse, is given us by St. Matthew in his seventeenth chapter. In the face of worn out people who had given in to the problem and who could see nothing more because they believed nothing more, Jesus cried out with a holy passion, "O faithless generation, how long must I be with you? O perverse people, how long must I bear with you?" Then he brought the healing that restored the tortured life to wholeness. His disciples asked Jesus why they could not do anything for the lad. Jesus told them that if they had faith as a grain of mustard seed they would say to a mountain — move over there! and it would. The image of the mustard seed as an image of faith can encourage us. It teaches us today that our faith may be tender indeed, but that it need not stay that way. Faith grows by the exercise of faith, by trusting God and acting upon the faithful vision of what we are to do as we meet all the circumstances of life ahead for us in the next seven days before we gather again.

Do not give in. Do not run away. Christ overcame death in order to give us faith to overcome the world that assaults us like the spring wind. We ask today, not to see the finished result of the future, but only for a faith that holds us firmly to God who brings us through to the future he has already shared with us in the Gospel of his Son.

Blessed are you, who have not seen and yet believe. Though now, for a little while, you may have to suffer various trials. But all this is for the proving of the genuineness of your faith. Without having seen Christ, you love him, and rejoice with a joy that is exalted. And the outcome of such a faith, is the salvation of your souls.

The Emmaus Stranger

This beautiful text from Luke 24 has inspired poets, musicians, artists, and above all — those who preach and hear the story of the risen Lord appearing to the two disciples as they walked from Jerusalem to the nearby town of Emmaus.

The evening hymn, "Abide with Me," is based upon this story. Rembrandt painted the picture of the two disciples with their guest at Emmaus. I have in mind another well-known painting that I have seen in many homes with the memorable scene of Jesus walking along side of the forlorn disciples as they journeyed on the evening of the Resurrection Day. Among all the resurrection accounts, this one of St. Luke's Gospel is surely among the best known and loved.

All of us enjoy being in a circumstance when we know something of importance that others do not. Luke uses this literary device as he narrates the events with extraordinary effectiveness.

". . . Their eyes were kept from recognizing him . . ." The evangelist is careful to make that point at the outset. It serves to caution us against too swift a judgment upon the pair who were astounded that this stranger knew nothing of all the things that had taken place in Jerusalem in the days immediately preceeding. What "kept their eyes from recognizing him"? Perhaps grief. Fear, no doubt. A great, crippling sense of let-down to be sure. But more than that. There is the hint of the Lord's own purpose in withholding instant recognition in his resurrection appearances. In all of the Gospels, no one knows him until he makes himself known. It is not as though people can come to the insight and full awareness of what his Resurrection means without his own empowering Spirit. Before his death and resurrection people could recognize Jesus. But afterward, no one knows him as Christ, the risen Messiah, until he speaks, breaks bread, or otherwise makes it possible for blind eyes to open.

This truth is meant to instruct and comfort us.

Those who saw the risen Lord do not stand in a position of special advantage over us. All of us have the same need — for God's Son to make himself known to our inmost hearts where faith is established. There is no superficial recognizing of Jesus as risen that would serve to cause momentary interest or satisfy a passing curiosity. We are not called to see Jesus as risen and then go on living as though nothing were changed. This is why the Emmaus disciples' eyes were held from truly seeing Jesus. Much more than seeing him is involved. It is to a new life and participation in a new creation that God calls us in his risen Son.

The text invites us to find ourselves with the two Emmaus disciples, seeing ourselves in their circumstances. That ought not be so difficult to do.

Who of us has not stored up great hopes in the heart, but then come to a point where everything about those hopes came crashing down? That is inevitable in life, of course. But the important point is that this story is not about life in general, but about hopes that were attached to God and centered in our expectations of how he would act for us in life situations. The disciples were caught up in the "if only" syndrome.

If only Jesus would have gone away from Jerusalem at the threatening hour of his betrayal and arrest. If only basic Roman justice could have prevailed in the face of the mob's shouting for his blood. If only Judas would not have betrayed the Master. If only Peter's defiance with the sword in the Gardon of Gethsemane could have sparked an immediate insurrection and Jesus could have been saved at the last minute. If only the women would not have gone to the tomb, and come back with this disturbing report of its being empty.

We all have our identity with this "if only" phrase which starts agonizing sentences.

If only I would have prayed more, believed more, done more — then my child would not have run out from behind the parked car and under the wheels of the oncoming traffic. If only I could have been more sensible and not so idealistic when falling in love and marrying the person who has made my life such a grinding misery and seemingly unending burden. If only I could have been told that those first tell-tale pains in the upper back were not a muscle sprain, but the vanguard of the runaway cancer cells that now have captured every vital organ in my body. If only I could have seen then what I know now.

We have endless ways of framing the "if only" sentences. It is not the intention of this sermon to denounce them and to stand at the comfortable distance this pulpit provides and point out how foolish and vulnerable we all are. I have my own experiences with the "if only" lamenting. We are all together at this point, even though the circumstances differ widely.

All of these "if only" thoughts, if left to dominate our minds and souls, keep Jesus Christ as a stranger. Behind them all lies one common denominator: the false idea that God is helpless with our folly and will do nothing in the face of our sin.

The text tells us that two disciples began the journey with heavy hearts and no subtle touch of resentment at the stranger walking with them who appeared to be so unpardonably uninformed.

But the point of the entire text is that this stranger does not want to remain a stranger. The heart of it is in his words, "Was it not necessary that the Christ should suffer these things and enter into his glory?"

He would not come to his Resurrection Day without enduring his suffering. He could not come to us in our loneliness and heartache, our remorse and our guilt, if he could not also tell us that he has visited those desolate stretches of our lives. He has come to bring us out of them, in the power of his own voluntary suffering and redeeming love. It is no longer necessary to live on the brink of despair, nor is it necessary to remain a captive of the forever-backward look upon life.

Our Lord Jesus Christ brings us forgiveness of sins here and now this day. Here is the gift that takes away the veil from our eyes, and lifts the fog of despondency from our hearts. He gave himself and is risen for us. The Gospel is the power that moves us from consternation at this stranger who does not seem to know what it means to lose a child, fail at work, suffer in marriage, worry about disease, to the incomparable wonder and joy in his presence as the opener of the word and the host at the table where he invites us.

We know Christ Jesus as the Savior and the reigning Lord of life as he makes himself known to us in the Gospel. The Scriptures are sacred and alive to us because they bear testimony to him. He is the living center of the Holy Book. Because he has made himself known to us in grace and mercy, the Bible is no longer about far away places and strange sounding names. It speaks to us because he speaks to us through it. It is his Word that reaches our hearts and makes us responsive to his grace and guidance for the living of the truth day by day.

We know Christ Jesus as the Savior and the reigning Lord as he comes to us through the Holy Supper. At Emmaus, he took the bread, gave thanks, broke it and gave it to the disciples. The verbs all fit the events of the Upper Room on the night of his betrayal. Christ's resurrection victory is shared with us through the meal he instituted with new meaning. He comes to us again and again in this wondrous way, inviting us to bring to him all our needs and everything within our souls that make us grateful. We speak of the Lord's Supper as a Holy Communion, a coming together with him and with each other that is indeed holy. We call this supper the Eucharist, which means a joyful giving of thanks. We call it a sacrament for it is a means of grace, a proclaiming of the Gospel that our sins are forgiven for the sake of Christ Jesus.

The disciples at Emmaus became messengers of this Lord rather than remaining distant from him as though he were a stranger. He made himself known to them; he makes himself known to us in the same way today — through the word of mercy and the meal of grace.

We sometimes walk through stretches of our lives when we are on this side of Emmaus, when the dominant force that moves us is the events of the past which turned out so differently than what we had hoped. But we do come to our own Emmaus-like destinations when our prayer for Jesus the Lord to abide with us is answered abundantly. In all of our journey, our walk is by faith. Our calling is to keep on trusting him, even when we can't discern his holy presence by the way things are turning out at the moment. But our eyes are not kept blind permanently. As we live with him and with his people, we keep getting our eyes opened. Though we do not see him now, we rejoice in him and believe in him. (1 Peter 1:8) And the outcome of our faith is the full and final revelation of his saving presence forever!

John Wesley put the final phrases of a hymn that is based on Psalm 23 in such a way that helps us retain the main themes of this text. Take it home with you and make room for it in your heart:

O may thy house be my abode,
And all my work be praise,
There would I find a settled rest,
While others go and come —
No more a stranger, nor a guest,
But like a child at home.

L'Chaim!

Our Jewish friends have a beautiful phrase in Hebrew that all of us might well take into our vocabulary.

"L'Chaim!" means "to life!"

It is a toast to life, a salute to the incredible miracle of being among the living. It is a word which recognizes life, rejoices in it, affirms it, and does so in such a way as to include the all-important note of celebration and appreciation.

Such a phrase suits us well as a title for this sermon on Jesus' sentence which breathes that joyful, affirmative spirit of the life which he grants to us by his rising again from the dead: *"I came that they might have life, and have it abundantly."* (John 10:10)

All Kinds of Symbols

Such a sentence has no small appeal to our mind and imagination as we try to picture the abundant life which is promised. We are not lacking for images from the world in which we live. The abundant life? Why of course! Mercedes Benz. Chevas Regal. Lakepoint Towers. These are symbols which come to mind quickly. And I do not mean to put them down. All are quality of the first order! But they symbolize something very different from the kind of abundant life our Lord offers.

The Spiritual Center

It would be a mistake to begin a line of thought which sharply divides the spiritual from the physical life we have from God. That is an old temptation into which the church has too often fallen. But, be that as it may, the abundant life which Christ himself is and which he provides is by no means a sum total of a list of all the best products which our consumer society enjoys. It begins with the soul within us, and reaches outward to embrace and sanctify the material blessings put into our hands.

81

The Setting of the Text

We can see this best by attending to the setting in which our Lord spoke this promise of the abundant life. As the ninth chapter of John explains, Jesus had healed a man who was blind from his birth. He opened those sightless eyes, so that a man who had never seen the beauties of life which delight the eye could savor and enjoy them in full. But this miracle was resented and opposed by the Pharisees — unbelievable as that seems! Jesus performed the miracle on the Sabbath day. In their eyes that made him an enemy of God and the religious establishment over which they held sway. And so they opposed him outright and put every pressure at their disposal on the man to renounce Jesus who had given him his eyesight!

With the grievous conflict in mind, then, Jesus points to the blind man who had received the gift of sight as an example of the healing and redeeming work God accomplishes through his Son — who came that they might have life and have it abundantly! And the deeper meaning of the miracle has to do with another kind of seeing, the vision of faith which can behold in Jesus Christ the one whom God sent, the one by whom grace and truth flow out to the whole world of humankind who need the mercy of God.

> *The thief comes only to steal and kill and destroy. I came that they might have life and have it abundantly.*
>
> (John 10:10)

The Gospel Is Power for Life

Jesus speaks of his messianic mission as the good shepherd who lays down his life for the sheep. The Pharisees threw the blind man out of the temple when he kept on insisting that his sight was returned to him by Jesus and that he now believed in him. The response Jesus made is centered on his concern not simply to have his claims accepted, but to be known and believed as the giver of life with God and to be followed for the sake of the nurture of that life. It's not just survival that God brings us through his Son. It is a restoring of the whole process of existence with God, guaranteed and sustained through his guidance, at the cost of his own life and certified by his rising from the dead.

When Religion Becomes Anti-Life

In taking measure of the forces which work against the life which God shares with us through the grace of his Son, we must not overlook the spirit of Pharisaism. That is a malady of spirit which can plague us, too. Another name for it is distorted religion. It is religion that has been drained of grace and mercy, which has hardened into rigid attitudes which exalt the decisions of humans in the church over the Gospel of God. Has that kind of religion ever affected you? It is a depressing experience! It happens whenever the Gospel of Christ's love is obscured. It is the picture of God that portrays him as against people, hateful of people, and always keeping scores on our sins so that we will surely pay in full. It is, in short, religion without grace. It is Christianity without Christ, and his shepherding care for our lost and wayward lives. It is the notion that God is forever dead-set against our ever having a moment of joy and genuine satisfaction.

I recall the story of the old Dutch preacher who served two congregations in Holland, one on either side of a dike. The only way he could get to both on winter Sunday mornings was to skate across the frozen body of water separating the two churches. When he asked permission of his ecclesiastical elders to skate the distance, they reluctantly agreed — but only on the stipulation that he would not *enjoy* doing so. That story illustrates a much larger problem, the problem of knowing God only under the Law and never under the Gospel. Don't let that blight cripple your spirit and rob your faith of the delighting in God, the enjoyment of his grace and abundant goodness.

Other Forces Sinned Against Life

Other forces do battle against the life which Christ gives us. I am thinking of our fellow member, Mr. Martin Wohlford who has been hanging onto life by the thinnest thread for nearly ten days now. He has been so dreadfully ill. This morning, as we bring him to the throne of grace in our prayers, we intercede for so many others who fill the hospitals and nursing homes of our land. The diseases which attack and ravage our bodies are severe reminders of the fallen world in which we live. Every ailment that cripples our bodies also inflicts fear upon our souls. And each time we are privileged to recover and regain our strength, it is a sign for us to read in faith. The sign points to him who is the healer and restorer of life.

Another of our members is entering his sixth week as an inmate of the county jail. This young man has more than physical problems to face as he awaits trial. He has to be on guard against physical assault, beatings, stabbings, and rape — all of which are threats from his fellow prisoners who crowd into filthy conditions that prevail in that overcrowded place of misery. This is what the mayor of Chicago ought to lay upon our consciences as citizens, the shame of our twentieth-century plight of prisoners. What does it matter if the Bears play their games downtown or out west in the suburbs? That is not a priority matter, unless we are indeed convinced that bread and circuses are the answer to our urban problems. All I am asking is that justice and basic rights of existence promised in our Constitution be given to prisoners. They are not provided now. I appeal to you to voice your protest and exercise your care for men and women who come out of our jails more hardened and more criminal than when they entered. If we mean what we say when talking about the goal of an improved quality of life, then there is no better place to apply that rhetoric to reality than in prison reform.

Shame on us for our misplaced priorities, our self-serving, our ingratitude for the gift of life, our contempt for it, our neglect of it!

Witness to the Abundant Life

Blessed are those who gently and quietly bear witness to us of the abundant life, who are in their own sincerity of faith and life a living embodiment of the pharse, "L'Chaim!" It isn't every Sunday that we have two couples who, together are celebrating nearly 120 years of marriage. Art and Emma Thoms, your sixty years of wedded life are a tesimony to the abundant life that God grants you so freely. Arnold and Emma Selle, your fifty-seven years of marriage are likewise a witness to the grace of Christ dwelling in your hearts and in your home. To both couples we say: best wishes! We hold you in great affection and respect, and this congregation has been blessed by your membership. God grant you his blessing in all the days ahead.

Life For Our Land

We have God to thank for the goodness he gives us in this land we call our own. Thinking of the quality of life once envisioned for the people of America, the old preacher John Winthrop had these words to say to those who first stepped off the boats from England to launch the great new venture:

. . . the only way to avoid shipwreck and to provide for our posterity is to follow the counsel of the prophet Micah, which is do justice, to love mercy, and to walk humbly with our God. For this end we must be knit together in this work as one man. We must entertain one another in brotherly affection. We must be willing to abridge ourselves of our superfluities for the supply of others' necessities. We must uphold the familiar commerce together in all meekness, gentleness, patience, and liberality. We must delight in each other. So shall we keep the unity of the Spirit in the bond of peace. And the Lord will be our God, and delight to dwell among us as his own people.

During this time as a nation, we have often strayed from these ideals. Those who have held up before us our national hypocrisies and errant ways ought not be driven off or silenced. They had best be listened to. And since we believe that we live by grace and not by works, it is fitting for us to renew our confidence and stir up our hopes for our land and our posterity in it. It is still a land of abundant life, richly blessed and lavishly endowed by God. We thank him for it. We ask for his pardon for our grievous sins. We seek his guidance for ourselves and all with whom we share life on the spaceship earth.

The church is still called to be that leaven in the world, to keep alive a springtime freshness in the souls of people as we point to him who is the life, and who came that we all might have that life of his, and have it abundantly.

A Place for You

Let not your hearts be troubled; believe in God, believe also in me. In my Father's house are many rooms; if it were not so would I have told you? And when I go and prepare a place for you, I will come again and will take you to myself, that where I am you may be also.

(John 14:1-3)

When Have You Heard These Words

Many of us have heard these words at another time and place. I have spoken them often to you in your living room, or when sitting at a kitchen table in your house on the occasion of the death of a loved one. Can you recall hearing them at such a time of crisis? It might be that nearly everything said and done in those first hours after a death of a family member or close friend is blocked out of our memory by the waves of shock that set in upon us in such moments. But I have also seen it happen that people listen as never before to a passage of Scripture such as this one when it is painfully clear that no word but Christ's word will truly reach and console the heart that is saddened by death.

In the Upper Room

These words which shed such a wondrous light of consolation upon us were first spoken in a dark time. It was on the night of his betrayal, when Jesus was in the Upper Room with the disciples — only a few hours before his own death, that he spoke these words to the disciples.

He was facing the final ordeal, not the disciples. Yet he comforted *them*, although they had no comfort to bring him. It is all so astounding when you recollect that scene! It is one more powerful testimony to Jesus Christ that he is the word made flesh, the incarnate Son of the heavenly Father who came to reveal to us that which is eternal.

87

The Father's House Is Spacious

Jesus speaks of the Father's house, the home of God, a place which he himself has prepared for life eternal. In his father's house are many rooms, or, as we learned it from the King James translation: "In my Father's house are many mansions . . ." Both words are appropriate: rooms or mansions. The point is the spaciousness, the ample, open, and eternal dwelling place that awaits God's faithful people after death has closed their eyes on this life. Such a magnificent future is in contrast to the present room in which the disciples and Jesus were gathered. Then and there the obvious thing was the temporary and the transitory, and that is the hallmark of everything temporal. We have here no abiding dwelling place. In this life the dwelling place given to God's Spirit in our own hearts is too often cramped and crowded in by our faithlessness, our distracted and self-serving spirit. It is a very basic biblical idea that salvation is best portrayed by a wide-open, uncluttered room. The Psalm writer of the Old Testament speaks of God's rescuing work as "setting his feet in a broad place." (Psalm 31:8) Jesus builds upon that word picture when speaking of the Father's house as many-roomed, as spacious and ample for a dwelling place that has no end.

The Personal Concern of Christ for Us

Even more important, however, than the emphasis upon the broad and capacious dwelling place that Christ has prepared, is the personal fellowship he promises in connection with eternal life. "I go to prepare a place for you . . . where I am, there you shall be also." That is so different from speaking in general terms about a vague "life after death" or the survival of the soul. The Scriptures tell us one thing clearly about our life with God in his house. We shall be there in the fellowship of his beloved Son, and when our bodies are raised from our own graves, we shall be like Christ our Lord and we shall see him as he is. (1 John 3:2-3) That is what counts, and that is all that we truly need to know. The Bible does not detail for us the landscape of heaven nor its furnishings. It points us to the all-important personal link with Jesus Christ. Who will be there? Who won't be there? What will we do? All these questions are natural enough, but they are questions that lead us astray from the main truth. No wonder, then, that God does not answer them! Leave all the rest to him; he will do all things well.

It's the person who makes the place, and gives us courage and confidence for entering that place. This is the central truth of this text and all that our Lord reveals to us of eternal life. I have an experience in mind that helps me in this regard and want to share it with you. When I was ten years old I distinguished myself one fine August day by falling headlong from one of those long, one-rope swings that boys love to rig up on tree branches.

I broke both arms, my nose, and remember a mouthful of Missouri mud and gravel in my teeth. There was nothing to do, of course, but to get me over to a nearby hospital, which my mother did with the help of a neighbor. That was a new place for me, with sights and smells and people very different from my little realm as a ten-year-old boy. I knew, of course, that all these professional-looking people in white were supposed to be there for my good. But that did not stop my heart from pounding. In fact, when the ether drops were being poured over the gauze covering my nose, I thought I was dying. But before losing consciousness under the anesthetic, I saw my father enter the room, come over to me, put his hand gently on my shoulder and say, "I'm here with you, son." Then everything was all right, for that voice and that face I knew and trusted. What a difference it made to me, in that place, that a person whom I knew and loved came to my side!

I think of that episode in my life when, from time to time, my thoughts turn toward death — my own as well as yours. In that inevitable moment, when no one can step into our shoes and do our dying for us, then we shall know in full what these words of Christ signify, "that where I am you may be also." It all stands upon his personal, caring, redeeming love for us. He calls us by name. In our baptism he makes his home in us. At the heart of our Christian faith it is a person-to-person bond which exists. In the ultimate matters of life, death, and eternity, our Lord speaks to us with the deepest level of personal concern. That is what eternal life is: belonging to him now and forever!

Eternal Life Is the Motive for Temporal Life

It has been a long-standing criticism of Christianity by some of its sharpest critics that eternal life is a giant aspirin tablet which is meant to blunt the person's awareness of harsh realities here and now. Classic Marxist orthodoxy holds such a view, and so do articulate people who are not Marxist but who deny the existence of God and his gift of eternal life which transcends death. Such criticisms can be understood in the light of church history, when there has been pie-in-the-sky escapism. But that hardly seems to be among the current maladies of the church. In fact, we might better be criticized for not holding forth the eternal perspective of the faith more ardently.

We might well pause, at least in thoughtful devotion, when we come to those great words of the Apostles' Creed which speak of the resurrection of the body and the life everlasting. It is a startling and revolutionary truth we proclaim. Among the great world religions there are numerous expressions of an after-life that is totally spiritualized. But our biblical faith proclaims the resurrection of the body. And if the living God cares so greatly for this body in which we house our earthly life that he wills to resurrect it and re-fashion it according to the glorified body of his Son, then we have all the reason we need to take care for the body. Here lies the Christian ethic, and the mainspring of our motive that leads us on to reach out in love for the helping of others in their needs as human beings here and now as well as beyond this life. The earliest Christian community recognized the material needs of the older widows and organized them to minister to those needs. Throughout the ages since, Christians have responded to the call of God to care for the body that will one day be resurrected. When this balance is struck, the criticism of Christianity as an opiate of the people cannot stand.

The Hope That Will Not Fail Us

Finally, these words of our Lord summon us to hold fast to the magnetic power of hope. The final test of that hope is our own death; that is the last chance the evil one has at us. What gives death it real sting is not just the anticipation of our heart and brain ceasing to function. It is the terminating of all the relationships, the endeavors, the activities, the dreams, and faithful striving that belong to our living. In the words of Psalm 103, it is the melancholy fear that when our life ends, "its place knows it no more." (v. 16) Christ's resurrection takes that fear and puts it out of the central place in our life. God does not forget his sons and daughters, and even though our great-grandchildren will know little or nothing about us and what we lived for, that does not matter. The place where we shall be is the place where Christ is present, and all our potential, all our sanctified hopes and dreams will be fulfilled in so great a measure that we have no words to describe it. Eye has not seen, nor has ear heard what good things God has prepared for those who love him. Christian hope makes it possible to look beyond the fulfillment of urgent wishes and pressing desires and offers a vision beyond suffering here and beyond our death.

This hope is not based on our self-confidence or upon any of our specific expectations of the future. It rests upon God's promise in his Son. This promise not only made Abraham travel to unknown territory; it is also the guiding motive for us who keep pointing to new life even in the face of corruption and death. Such a hope prevents us from clinging to what we have and frees us to move away from the safe place as we enter unknown and fearsome territory. When we walk in the valley of the shadow of death, that good and gracious shepherd of our souls will be our faithful guide. We can go our way, then, also over that final path, with songs of peace and gladness in our hearts.

A century ago John Henry Newman wrote an evening prayer which expresses well the whole spirit in which we see the present in the light of that place which Christ has prepared for us:

> *Support us, O Lord, all the long day of this troubled life until the shadows lengthen, and the evening comes, when the busy fever of life is hushed, and our work is done. Then in thy mercy grant us a safe lodging, a holy rest, and peace at the last, through Jesus Christ our Lord. Amen*

Desolate No More

I will not leave you desolate; I will come to you.

(John 14:18)

Preparing a Family to Live On Well Supplied

Nearly two decades have passed since Kent Knudsen died of a rare brain disease. This gifted churchman, the president of a major Lutheran Church body, while yet in his forties, was in the final stage of critical illness. He gathered his family around him in the hospital room in Minneapolis while he yet had strength and clarity of mind to speak to them of that which he wanted them to have.

He said, "May you be strengthened with all power according to Christ's glorious might, for all endurance and patience with joy, giving thanks to the Father, who has qualified us to share in the inheritance of the saints in light. He has delivered us from the dominion of darkness and transferred us to the kingdom of his beloved Son, in whom we have redemption, the forgiveness of sins." One can imagine the power of such a moment, as Knudsen spoke the words from Colossians 1 to prepare his family for the time when he would no longer be with them.

Such an act of preparing people to carry on after one's own death is an act of love. It reveals the forethought of one about to take leave; it discloses the awareness of the needs of others who will need to face desolate times with inner reserves sufficient for such testing.

Jesus' Promise to His Own

The Gospel reading for today gives us Jesus' words preparing his disciples for what was immediately at hand. In the Upper Room on the night before his crucifixion, he was in the company of his betrayer, denier, and all the rest of the twelve who deserted him at the Cross. In that time and place

91

he had his own ordeal of pain before him; the specter of his own death could not be brushed aside.

Yet his words are full of love and care and preparation for the disciples. Everything we read in chapters thirteen through seventeen of John's Gospel are words of the Lord for the church. He promises the coming of the Holy Spirit to be the advocate and comforter of the disciples who are caught up in their own desolation on that foreboding night. The heart of his message to them is this: "I will not leave you desolate. I will come to you."

The Empowering Spirit of Christ Jesus

Disciples then and now need help in understanding how it happens that this promise of Christ is kept: "I will come to you. I will not leave you desolate."

The keeping of the promise is through the sending of the Holy Spirit at the intercession of Jesus to the heavenly Father. Jesus names the Spirit as the Counselor. In the King James version, the Comforter. At the heart of the original word (paraclete) is our word — Advocate. The Holy Spirit pleads our cause before the throne of grace. He speaks for us. He tells the Father of the saving work of Jesus Christ for us. It is the Spirit who not only takes our cause before the judgment seat of God. He also brings life to the Gospel in our own hearts. The Spirit works in many mysterious ways, but the sure and steady way he always works is through the Holy Gospel which tells us of Christ's Cross and Resurrection as the great work accomplished for us. That message is the heart of what we preach, in and out of season. That message is at the heart of the sacraments of Baptism and the Eucharist. You and I are gathered here today in one congregation, and we are united with all believers, through the Spirit's power. Christ's words, "I will not leave you desolate, I will come to you," are the spirit's gift to us again today. This sermon not only talks about that gift. It offers the gift. Hear the good news with an open heart. It is no longer necessary that your life or mine be surrounded and held in by the desolation of sin.

Feeling Desolate

Do we know what we are talking of when speaking that word "desolate"?

Desolation calls to mind an abandoned house against a bleak landscape. It imparts the feeling of loneliness, isolation, futility. But we need to be able to distinguish between the feeling of desolation and the fact of it.

A child of five feels desolate on the first day of kindergarten. When mother leaves, that youngster is surrounded by new sights and sounds. But that feeling of desolation, strong and real as it is, ends. There is life after the first day of kindergarten! And so the feeling of being suddenly desolate gives way to the assurance that the new situation is good indeed.

Or follow in the camera of your mind to a man in his 80s. He still lives in the family house which has been home for over fifty years. Alone now, he nods in front of the television as Dan Rather reports the evening news. The half-eaten TV dinner is cooling on the tray stand beside him. He awakens with an audible sigh. Life alone in a large house, much too much for him to take care of, is lonely. But that feeling in him is not the only thing or the main thing about his life. His eye moves from the news report to the mantle, which is filled from end to end with pictures of children, grandchildren, great-grandchildren — at the center position is the picture of the woman with whom he shared six decades of life. Lonely in moments like this, he is not abandoned. The children come to visit, and when the distance is too great, they do call. They care. He's loved and he knows it. That lonely feeling is side by side with faith and gratitude. He knows the presence of the heavenly father in the house. He looks forward to tomorrow; a grandchild is coming by to do the lawn. Life could be worse — far worse. The feeling of loneliness is not connected to the face of desolation.

Being Desolate

As Jesus said, "I will not leave you desolate," he meant I will not leave you orphaned. To be orphaned is not a feeling only; it is a devastating, tragic fact.

Being orphaned (the Greek word in John 14:18 is the basis of our English term orphan) as Jesus used it in connection with the disciples after his crucifixion means above all to be left alone with our sins. Desolate is the fact of a lifestyle separate from the merciful presence of God. That fact comes home to people forcefully, in spite of the efforts to shut it out with diversions and rationalizations of every sort.

I think of a father who sets aside the First Commandment for years and years. His life is centered in business success. He is successful. I can't even imagine the kind of wealth he amasses. Throughout his waking hours money is the dominant thing in his life; his worship of this idol is truly awesome. It is 6:45 p.m. on a late spring evening. His eleven-year-old son is at the plate in a Little League game, and connects squarely with a pitch. He makes it all the way around and crosses home plate in triumph. The father, having just arrived in business suit and brief case from the fourth successful business negotiation of that day, waits at the bench to greet the young hero. Their eyes meet. As the Dad slaps the boy on the back and gives him a hug, the lad's body stiffens. It's not that he's embarrassed to be embraced with all the other kids looking. The boy lives with an inner hurt and anger that even he does not fully understand; all he knows is that the father always has other priorities. He knows his place — it's after all the other things get the best time, the best energies, the best interests of that father. Feeling his son stiffen against his body, the father gets the message, lets loose, steps back, turns away, and walks slowly to the car. His own eyes fill suddenly with tears as he wants to blame the kid, the pressures, the work, the need to provide. But the bottom line fact is his desolation. Truly he is orphaned. The spectacular rise in business profits is a merciless master. When it is elevated to the center of life around which all else revolves, it yields no blessing. All it offers is the relentless pressure to make next month's or next year's report look even better. That is desolation.

I have known her since she was a child. Even then she dressed for grade school as though she was twice her years. Not many girls in the sixth grade wore glass high heels to school on promotion day. She's gifted. And she has a great capacity to love and to care. But she has chosen to channel it all in her own way to those who keep using her like a detachable, throwaway wrapper. Over and over again she has bemoaned her loneliness, and more recently her full disgust with all this talk about the grace and goodness of the Lord. She lives in a luxury condo, where she has provided bed and board for numerous men over the years. The man who is now living with her is ten years her junior; they both know that when he has finished his graduate schooling he will leave her. My plea to her and to him is to recognize the desolation of the whole situation. She looks across the ornately decorated living room at me with eyes that could not be changed by the cosmetic surgery she recently underwent. A face lift will not fix sad eyes, that look out on a world that seems as desolate as the wasteland of the empty soul behind those eyes. My heart goes out to her. I am her pastor. My word to her is simple, "It doesn't have to go on this way. There can, there really can, be a different way to live." I speak to her and wait for the words to someday be believed — in the name of Jesus Christ who said, "I will not leave you desolate." But her fanatical clinging to the shell of relationships that always break is itself heartbreaking. Whatever one sows, one reaps. That is written so deeply in those eyes of hers that I cannot forget.

Grace in the Worst Moment

Jesus' promise of an end to desolation was made in the worst moment for the disciples. He pointed beyond their desolation to his future for them and with them in the presence of the Holy Spirit. He is never willing to let us write our own epitaphs as though our own loneliness, futility, rebellion, were the last truth about our existence. The disciples could not believe Jesus that night in the upper room. He spoke to them but they had no capacity to grasp the new realm his resurrection would bring. Today, it isn't that people don't want to be loved or cared for or treated justly. It is that people can't believe that they deserve such treatment for themselves and they distrust it when offered to others.

But grace is grace. It is not as though we can demonstrate our worthiness for desolation to end. We can't. But it is no longer necessary for us to hang onto our feeling of unworthiness or to guess whether God will be satisfied with our transitory, fragmented and fragile responses to him. That always leads to the suspicion that if God or others *really* knew me, he and they could no longer accept me, love me, and fill that inner desolation with confidence and peace.

This Gift Is Yours

Let grace be grace. He offers you and me again today, here and now, what he has done for us. It all rests upon his work for us, not ours for him. He comes to us in the message of sin forgiven, of bleak landscapes of life now given the cross at the center. That is the miracle of his love for us and for all sinners. It is the love which bears, believes, hopes, and endures all things. Take it, please, in faith and open your heart to this gift of unsurpassed worth.

Many things follow, that have to do with fruitful living. But the main thing this sermon proclaims, the one thing Christ promises through this text is fundamental to all those other gracious and welcome things happening: you are desolate no more!

That They May Be One

Holy Father, keep them in thy name, which thou hast given me, that they may be one, even as we are one.

(John 17:11)

Concerning Unity

The truth we hear today concerns the oneness of the people of Christ. If I would ask you this simple question, "Are you for the unity of Christians?" there would be no doubt in my mind that all of you present would answer yes.

If I could ask you another question, ". . . and would you be willing to die for the cause of unity among Christians?" I would anticipate a very different response. It is one thing to agree to the desirability of Christian unity. It is quite another to lay down one's life for that cause.

You and I are not called upon to lay down our lives so that believers in Christ Jesus could be one. That has already been done for us. Our task is to hear this great word of our Lord and receive the gift he brings with it, to us and to his people everywhere. He prayed that we all might be one. And then he left the Upper Room in Jerusalem where the disciples were gathered with him to hear this prayer. Out of the city walls he went that dark night of his betrayal, across the Brook Kidron to the Garden of Gethsemane, then to a shameful travesty of a trial before the high priest, then to sentencing before Pontius Pilate, and then to Calvary where he suffered the agonies of the crucifixion and breathed his last — in order that this prayer might rise up to the throne of God with the full, earnest appeal of the Son of God that the petition be granted.

When Jesus Prays

"That they might be one, even as we are one . . ." These few, simple words open up a vast and holy meaning to us. When Jesus prayed these words, it was not like our prayers. All of us know that our prayers are limited by our human boundaries. Distractions enter in. Our prayers drift. We fall asleep. Or we pray rarely, much too rarely. But not so with the Lord Christ. His mind and will were one with the Father. His vision of what to pray for was uncluttered by all the narrowing forces that cramp our souls. His communion with God was complete and free. In praying that all those given him by the Father might be one Jesus came to the Father with an intensity and earnestness that is revealed by the cross he was willing to carry for us all. It is our Lord who prays! And that makes all the difference in the outcome of the prayer.

Prayer, Not a Flow Chart

It is a *prayer* that we hear. Jesus does not give us a blueprint for an organization, complete with hierarchy, prestige, and all the things that can confuse about the unity of the church. He prays. The unity of God's people is centered in his prayer. Christ himself is the unity that holds us all together as a people forgiven. Prayer is an action of the soul; it is the response to God that arises out of faith. Prayer is centered in God. He is the object of faith, not the church or even the most exemplary strategies for unifying Christians.

This cannot be emphasized too strongly: the unity of believers in Christ is commparable to a living organism rather than organization. The New Testament Scriptures speak of unity in ways that correspond to Jesus' high priestly prayer: a living body with widely differing members, a flock under one shepherd, branches attached to a single vine. The heart of unity lies in our oneness with Christ himself. That intimate, dynamic spiritual union with the risen Savior never leaves us disembodied. We are drawn to each other because he has first drawn us to himself and has given us his redeeming love.

Think of the prayer of Christ being answered now and continually, until the end of time. Think of it being answered on four levels.

Level One: Time Joined with Eternity

The first is the unity of Christians now alive in earth with the faithful of God who are secure in his heavenly presence. This facet of unity is neglected too often. Change that. One of the most wonderful ways we experience this level of unity with the church triumphant is through hymnody and the rich heritage of worship. In our hymnal we have a hymn from the fourth century ("That Easter Day with Joy Was Bright"). Another hymn was written by Thomas à Kempis some five hundred years ago. The writers of these and other texts and melodies rest in Christ's peace. Yet their work crosses over the boundaries of time and blesses us again today. The hymnal is a treasure of witness to the unbroken lines of faith and worship which death itself cannot break.

Level Two: Denomination to Denomination

Another level at which the prayer of Christ is being answered is that of church body to church body. We welcome word on the labors of faithful church leaders to attend to matters of doctrine and practice that have to do with Christ's reign among his people. When separated Christians draw closer, speaking the truth in love to each other, the prayer of Christ is being answered. The Holy Spirit sends us people of great vision for this task. It is hard work, for we become comfortable and stubborn in our settled denominational forms.

But denominations in and of themselves are not the problem. Our making them the end instead of the means is the problem. Earlier in this century the Christian church was greatly blessed with people of rare vision and spiritual tenacity in wrestling with the problems of sinful division in the church. These include names such as William Temple, John R. Mott, Willem Visser t'Hooft, and D. T. Niles. Under the leadership of the Holy Spirit, they moved the church to a new urgency for unity in response to Christ's prayer, and mission to the world as the purpose of unity. Today we add new names to this number: Lesslie Newbiggen, Desmond Tutu, T. K. Ting, and Herbert Chilstrom. Each bears witness to the unity that must find expression amidst Christians who suffer persecution, who are led into new organizational expressions of unity, and who are participants in the world mission of the Gospel.

Level Three: Congregation to Congregation

Our Lord's intercession for unity reaches us at the level of congregation to congregation. Soon we will call a new assistant pastor here at Grace Church. This, and every time a congregation calls a minister, involves us in the prayer of Christ. We don't raise up our own pastors and other ministers of the Gospel in our own congregation. Congregations band together to establish seminaries and other training centers for those called to service in the church. We are grateful for the unity that is necessary for this work to go on, and see it as one more sign of God's answering the petition his Son brought before him. A few days ago, four neighboring pastors were our guests for thought, prayer, and planning for more cooperative ministry in which we all share. Our bonds of unity with other congregations begin nearby and stretch worldwide, as we support one another with people, money, and prayer.

Level Four: Christian to Christian

"That they may be one" is being answered by the heavenly Father as we respond to his grace in the person-to-person encounters that are a part of our daily experience. This can be overlooked or underrated, but it must not be put aside as of little significance in the grand design of the oneness of the people of God. Several instances come to mind.

I was on the station platform awaiting a train from Yokohama to Tokyo one fall morning when I noticed a man who seemed a bit lost. I spoke to him, and his beautiful Scottish burred accent made me glad I did. We struck up a conversation as we boarded the right train for the destination we had in common. It turned out that he was a Presbyterian missionary *en route* home to Scotland after years of Christian service in China and Southeast Asia. His boat had docked in Yokohama, and he had a day to look around before sailing off for home. He told me some wonderful stories about this vocation, and seemed interested in everything around him. I recall his commenting especially on the Japanese university students who were on the train with us. He took their black uniforms and white plastic collars to be seminary garb! I regretted to correct his impressions, but he took it with good humor and enjoyed a laugh on himself.

As we came to the Tokyo Central Station we got off together and shook hands before parting. He took my hand firmly in his own and said, "We'll meet again, you know . . ." I thought about his sentence as I went on to my appointment. Where will we meet? Not in Japan. Nor in Scotland or the U.S.A. No, we will meet again in the church triumphant as we all gather about the throne of God to praise him forever! This hour in my life occurred thirty-seven years ago, but it will stay with me always. I cite it to stir your own awareness of those splendid, unplanned moments that bring you into the presence of another person of the faith. Such moments express the unity for which Christ prayed and they are unforgettable.

Another sign of the answered prayer came much more recently and under quite different circumstances. I was hurrying to an appointment in downtown Chicago recently, fighting time and losing the battle. I came to the intended place but had to drive several more blocks to find a parking lot. Wincing at the sight of what it costs to park there, I whizzed in and found an empty spot in the lot. No sooner did I have one foot out of the car when the attendant yelled at me to get my car out of there — or else! I yelled right back at him my idea that this parking spot was just fine. Like two banty roosters we raised the decibel levels as we got angrier with each other. He finally moved my car to some unknown place while I raced to meet the people awaiting me.

Three hours later I came back to that parking lot, hoping not to see the person with whom I had the senseless shouting match. There he was, as big as Goliath, standing menacingly in the parking lot office. I went straight up to him. "Look, I'm sorry for blowing my top at you," I said. He came right back with, "And I am, too." I asked him if he was a Christian. He said he was. Then, I suggested, why don't we shake hands here and now as befits two brothers in Christ. His black hand and my white hand met, and something more than a handshake was symbolized there. This tiny episode in the huge universe that evening did not in itself mend the woes of the human family. But it is connected to the One whose hands were folded for us and then crucified for our sins and the woes of the whole world.

Every Christian Counts

Never denigrate the modest events of daily life in which reconciliation, love, and divine grace win the day over hositility, hate, and mutual neglect. Cherish every one of them. Let them multiply. All together as well as individually they bear witness to the prayer of Christ Jesus that the oneness he shares with the Father might be reflected in the oneness he makes possible among us who bear his name.

For the Sake of the World

This oneness is for the sake of the world. Our holding together in faith and love is so that the world can catch on to the plans God has for the whole creation! We are on our way into the vast and unbreakable unity that God wills, and for which his Son died. It is not our doing. It is his gift. Open your eyes in faith to the levels at which this unity is given to us: time and eternity, denomination to denomination, congregation to congregation, person to person. God be praised for such a gift!

The Miracle
of an Opened Mind

*Then he said to them, "These are my words which I spoke to you, while
I was still with you, that everything written about me in the law of Moses
and the prophets and the psalms must be fulfilled." Then he opened their
minds to understand the Scriptures, and said to them, "Thus it is written,
that the Christ should suffer and on the third day rise from the dead, and
that repentance and forgiveness of sin should be preached in his name and
forgiveness of sins should be preached in his name to all nations, beginning
from Jerusalem. You are witnesses of these things. And behold, I send the
promise of my Father upon you; but stay in the city, until you are clothed
with power from on high." Then he led them out as far as Bethany, and
lifting up his hands he blessed them. While he blessed them, he parted from
them. And they returned to Jerusalem with great joy, and were continually
in the temple blessing God.*

(Luke 24:44-53)

Ascension on Our Minds

The miracle of Christ's Ascension keeps on unfolding. Not only is our Lord
risen. Not only in his risen form did he appear in the presence of the disciples and eat some broiled fish with them — thus assuring them that he was
not a mirage.

But also this, ". . . he opened their minds . . ."

That is no small part of the miracle of the ascended Lord's power, that
minds once closed to Christ are opened. That is the sentence from today's
Gospel that we now come back to:

*Then he opened their minds to understand the Scriptures, and said to them,
"Thus it is written, that the Christ should suffer and on the third day rise
from the dead."*

103

What a Work of the Creator!

The mind is such an astounding part of our bodies. Some time ago I had an experience in this connection which I wish all of you could share. I watched a neuro-surgeon perform an operation on the brain. The patient was a young man in his early 30s, suffering from a tumor deep into the core of the brain. Step by step the preparation proceeded, until the area of the skull immediately over the diseased section was opened and laid back. Then it was visible — the brain. It is a sight to inspire awe. I mention it to you for that reason, not to make our stomach queasy at the thought. The brain is the most complex of all the things that God has created; nothing in the entire universe can match it. The brain weighs just over three pounds I am told. It can be held in one hand. Yet there are literally billions of cells and cell connections within it, imparting via chemical and electrical transmission all our thought, all our feelings, all our motives, all our drives, all our sensations. Think of it: nothing is ever said or done in all the world on any given day but that it does not first originate in a brain.

What a miracle the mind is!

Open to Christ Through the Scriptures

But more than that — what a miracle takes place when a mind is opened to the scriptures. And even more than that — what a supreme work of God it is when the mind is opened by the Lord Christ to the spiritual understanding of what he is saying to us through the Holy Scriptures.

I think of all those billions of brain cells responding to the Spirit's mysterious drawing power. The picture in my mind is that of a gentle wind that blows across a mountain valley with countless aspen leaves responding to that invisible breath which we call wind. Yet it happens. And at a deeper level, it happens that the resurrection gospel is spoken to people now even as the announcement of the great deed was spoken to disciples whom St. Luke describes. And the mind opens!

It Comes from God's Side

What opens the mind is not a sudden flash of intellectual genius, nor the discovery of some hidden truth that unfolds because of hard thinking from our human side. The miracle of an opened mind is that of God's initiating.

Christ the Savior has come, has suffered, has been raised, and now rules as Lord of all. The Gospel is put upon the lips of human beings. As the news of our redemption from sin is faithfully spoken, Christ comes to his people. He opens our minds. He does so through the scripturally-formed testimony that has come down to us from the apostles whom he chose so long ago.

The Center Is Christ

. This is how we are to receive the Scriptures, as witness to the grace of God in Christ Jesus. From Moses onward in the Old Testament, up through the prophets and the Psalms, the whole story of Israel's destiny under God comes to its fulfillment in Jesus the Christ. The New Testament bears its witness, through Gospels, Acts, Epistles, and the final glimpse of the end of history in the Revelation given to St. John — all these words come to fruition in a person. Not a theory or a doctrine or even a church body. The Scriptures are fulfilled in the living, risen Christ of God! He stands at their center. The words of the Bible are all given in order to point to the living Word, our Lord Jesus himself.

When we say that God is our refuge and strength, or that God is the shepherd who leads us in paths of righteousness, we bring these familiar passages in their fulfillment in the One who speaks to us with mercy for our sins and power for renewed lives. The dark passages of the Bible which puzzle us we also bring to him who said, "I am the light . . ." The judgments of God which come upon us because of our sins, altogether justified in holding us accountable for our transgressions, give way to the Gospel of Christ's suffering for our sins. Here is the key which opens the Bible and makes it a living word — the key is the resurrected Lord.

Dividing What God Has Joined

Great harm is done when the Bible is separated from the risen Lord to whom it points.

Our time has enough sad instances of people waging bloody war in the name of the Bible. The centuries before our own tell too many similar stories of tragic misuse of the Bible. Worldwide fundamentalism is constantly making this mistake. The Bible is used to support apartheid, to condone bloody governmental coups, to pit Catholic and Protestant against each other, to justify one economic class above another. But all this happens because minds remain closed to Christ. In spite of all the pious talk about the Bible, if it is closed to Christ and his redeeming love, it is closed indeed.

Too often in our time the illusion is spread that people who quote the Bible are people of closed minds. Their prejudices stand out all over the place. A stubborn, narrow, carping, and judgmental spirit hangs like a pall over them. All this is a denial of the very heart of what the Bible proclaims. It is a caricature and we must have no part in it.

Open-minded Christians are known by humility, willingness to repent, patience with people who are at the bottom of the heap, adaptability to those who are entirely different, readiness to bear witness to Christ when asked, standing securely on the sure ground of the Gospel, acceptance of people regardless of their color, religion, economic standing, etc. In short, open-minded means Christ-minded. The Scriptures give us the framework for that gift. Does the Bible put blinders on the mind? Not when Christ is the living center of that Word! Think of Isaiah 61, and the vision of God's reign to all corners of the earth. Or the book of Jonah with its proclamation of the universal love of God. Or the book of Job with its profound probing into the mystery of human suffering. Or the opening verses of the Gospel of John with such a breathtaking sweep of movement of the eternal God into our flesh. Or the thirteenth chapter of 1 Corinthians with its proclamation of the supremacy of divine love in all the relationships of life. These passages and all the others which come to us in the Bible culminate in the risen Savior. This is our Ascension faith. Christ is the power to open our minds to the Easter book of our faith, and center us among the Easter people of God.

Faithful Use of the Mind

We are called to love God with our mind. That means respect for the intellect, and obedience in putting our brains to work on the hard questions that vex, challenge, and interest people in our time. The church must *out-think* the secular world. To do so, minds must be open and responsive as good stewards of the Creator's gifts. Too often the church is seen otherwise, as the haven of escape from hard questions. The Gospel we proclaim, to be sure, is simple and straight-forward. It must always be powerful because it is clear, whether to a tiny child or a Nobel laureate. What is complex is the life situation to which we address the Gospel. Connecting faith and life is demanding as well as exciting. Remember that this congregation is the place where people with long-term illness come together regularly and wrestle with the hard questions of the struggle. Their minds are open to the varied ways and times of the Lord's healing care. More recently a group of people in business life have formed another group that is addressing the demanding issues of relating fatih and daily life in the marketplace. Our lawyers meet once a month to do the same. Medical professionals have been active in similar pursuits. All these and many more events in the life of the congregation tell of minds being opened to the calling of the risen Lord to follow him into the world.

Much Contested Ground

The mind is a battle ground between forces in open rebellion against God.
The whole drug culture is based upon a bid for the mind. Enormous amounts of money are paid for drugs that make people dependent upon chemical substance. After the mind expands through drug-induced sensations, there follows the crash into depression and the vacuum of demonic dependency.

The mind is assaulted by workaholism and its chain of money, power, and status as the goal of life. The mind is cluttered by an ever-increasing tide of catalogs, brochures, and every kind of junk mail that fills our mailboxes. The mind can be swallowed up by consumerism. The mind is straight-jacketed by tensions and the pressures of worry about everything from nuclear holocaust to a faltering marriage or runaway children. From every side the mind is beleaguered by incessant forces which seek to own it. It's no surprise. Once the mind is owned, all else follows.

Ascension for the Mind

In the face of all this, behold the ascended Christ! "He opened their minds . . ." and he still does and he will ever do so. The most important space there is can still be found not among the far reaches of the universe, but the space between our ears. The mind belongs to God. He created it. He lifted it from the dominion of darkness when he raised his Son from death. The mind is his dwelling place in the Spirit. Let it be open to his dear Son, the living Word, whose ascension song of triumph blends into one all the varied themes of the Bible to make it our own song of salvation.

The Promise
and the Task

*Now the eleven disciples went to Galilee, to the mountain to which Jesus
had directed them. And when they saw him they worshiped him; but some
doubted. And Jesus came and said to them, "All authority in heaven and
on earth has been given to me. Go therefore and make disciples of all nations, baptizing them in the name of the Father and of the Son and of the
Holy Spirit, teaching them to observe all that I have commanded you; and
lo, I am with you always, to the close of the age."*

(Matthew 28:16-20)

Meaning, Not Details

The evangelist Matthew does not describe the event of the Ascension of Jesus. Rather, as the celebrated text we have just heard shows, he gives us
its meaning. This is what the ascension of our Lord proclaims: the fullness
of the divine authority to rule has been given to the resurrected and ascended Son of God.

That is the promise: "All authority has been given to me . . ." as Jesus
told the gathered disciples in Galilee.

And this is the task: "Go and make disciples of all nations, baptizing
them in the name of the Father and of the Son and of the Holy Spirit."

Left with a Promise

The Ascension left the disciples, as it also leaves the church of all the
ages, with nothing to rely on but the promise of God: the promise of the
coming of the Holy Spirit, the promise of our Lord's being with his own,
the promise of his coming again in a way that would be visible and glorious. Now, no more seeing and nothing to go on with but his word, they
were to make disciples of all nations, baptizing and teaching as Jesus com-
missioned them.

As we celebrate the Ascension of Jesus, let this promise be at the center of our whole sense of the event and its meaning for us. We have no interest in cosmology, levitation, angels, and other diversions. Attending to the meaning of the ascension does not set Christ light years away from us. As Luther put it, "the right hand of God is everywhere . . ." Believing Jesus Christ to be at the Father's right hand is believing that his promise to be present wherever his own gather is valid and trustworthy.

Ours by Faith

And so the ascension of Christ is a truth that stands in line with all the revealed truth of God: it is ours in faith. We trust God's reliability altogether. We fit this truth to the glowing center which the Gospel is. He completed his saving work for the world and presents it to the heavenly Father as the capstone of our redemption. The ascension does not make us star-gazers. It declares us forgiven by Christ and called to the task he has for the church.

The Ways of His Coming

We must learn with the disciples. Some doubted. Some worshiped Jesus. Our learning from Christ cannot be with selecting this truth but crossing another out. We really are not spectators. This is not the option for disciples.

The Ascension has taken place! And the result is the empowering Spirit of Christ upon us to cause us to lift up our heads to him. He is with us in his words and with the water, the wine and bread. By way of them he is present and gives of himself and his gifts.

And there are still more tangible ways in which Jesus makes himself known to us as the ascended one. By word and sacrament we are made alive and energized. This life and energy are not just intended to spin us around and around inside ourselves. Jesus makes himself known through us as we are little Christs to our neighbor, whom he has appointed to receive our service as his substitute. Whatever we do for one another he takes as done to himself. "I was hungry and you gave me food." "When did we see you hungry?" "Truly I say to you, as you did it to one of the least of these my brothers and sisters, you did it to me." These words from the Savior's parable in Matthew 25 belong in our ascension worship and our ascension awareness.

The Task Given

The task Jesus left us is enormous. Sometimes the equipment seems derisory. Yet that is what Jesus left us with, and there is no more reliability about it than Jesus himself.

We come together to celebrate Christ's Ascension as people who have found him reliable, or with the hope that maybe that reliability is in our lives without which everything flows uncertainly in relativity, fads, points of view, fashions of mind. Take hold of what he has left us. He has left us in our humanity lifted up to the Father's presence, no longer trapped in the downdraft of fate or the inevitability of defeat. We have his promise. We have his word. Him we do not see, but we hear his word and we see his love at work in the lives of those who belong to him in faith. We are baptized. We come to his table. Thus he brings us his gifts which look so small, so unavailing. But *Christ* comes through these means and that is what makes them powerful and alive forevermore.

Beyond Division to Unity

Our fractured world is in desperate need for the uniting and reconciling love which triumphed in the ascension of Christ. The Ascension draws us to Christ, and to each other. Let no barrier keep you from the others in the Christian body because of external things such as skin color, economic standing, gender, national difference, political preference, or age difference. All across the face of the earth there are congregations of baptized people who say yes to the ascension. We need to find each other and say yes to each other. Our hands must be joined, because our hearts are united in Christ.

This can happen in ways that are of deep significance. Several years ago, on a sabbatical pastoral journey that took me around the world in contact with fellow Christians, I experienced the power of Christ to hold people together when no other force will do it. We did not know each other beforehand. But with the arrangements in place that enabled us to know each other, it was remarkable how quickly the boundaries of language, class, etc. were crossed. In the years following, these beginnings have been continued through the visits of overseas Christians to us and through correspondence and sharing of our blessings.

With Hope for the Completion

This is the most direct way I know of for Christians to bring the ascension power to bear in such a way as to heal the dangerous suspicions and alienations that keep us apart.

We do not see through the cloud that surrounded him at his ascension. Yet he is not on the other side of that cloud; he is on our side. His word, his promise, his task — as we enter into all these we know his presence and share it with others. He enables and guides, fitting things together for blessing for his people. He exercises the loving power of God for us as he is at the Father's right hand. In his love for us he gives us to serve and to suffer for his sake and the Gospel's, and to win his victories in the world.

When the last victory is won, we see him.

And in seeing him face to face, in company of all his people of all time and place, our blessed Lord brings the whole saving plan of God to completion!

About the Author

For a recent book he wrote on preaching, Dean Lueking used the subtitle "The Art of Connecting God and People." The phrase aptly describes Lueking's sense of what preaching is — calling, gift, art, and nothing less than a lively connecting of God with people in all aspects of human life.

Serving with one congregation for three and one half decades, Grace Lutheran Church in River Forest, Illinois, he has had opportunity to marvel at the patience and forbearance of people in the congregation who hear him preach, weekly and sometimes weakly, for more than a third of a century. But the fact that both preacher and congregation continue to thrive is itself testimony to where the power lies in preaching. As the witness is set forth to the towering sufficiency of the risen Christ, and as that witness is placed side by side with life as people live it, the results are inspiring.

During the two years before his ordination in 1954, he spent two months in Japan. The experience has given him a continuing world perspective on congregational significance and preaching. He has traveled to Europe, the Middle East, and the Orient several times to listen to and learn from Christians abroad. Such experiences continue to enrich his preaching and enliven his pastoral work.

At various times in recent decades, earnest voices have claimed that preaching is in real trouble. What is rightly in trouble, this preacher contends, is faithless, careless pulpit work that should be judged for what it is. But the proclamation of the risen Lord, offered with passion for people and deep commitment to their good is not in trouble. When all else passes away, this Word continues. Based on that conviction, these sermons are written.